10 Things Your Mama Should Have Told You

Lessons for Cultivating an Extraordinary Life

Dr. Evelyn Collins

10 Things Your Mama Should Have Told You: *Lessons for Cultivating an Extraordinary Life*
First Published by Onyx Productions NYC
Copyright Dr. Evelyn Collins 9/2023

All rights reserved. No portions of this book may be reproduced, stored in a retrieval system, or transmitted in any form or by any means – electronic, mechanical, photocopy, recording, scanning, or other – excerpt for brief quotations in critical reviews or articles, without the prior written permission on the publisher.

For more information, email onyxprodnyc@gmail.com
First edition September 2023
Published in New York, New York, by Dr. Evelyn Collins, Onyx Publishing Company.
Cover Designed by James Edward Alexander (Photo) and Vincent Miller (Graphics)

Library of Congress Copyright 9/4/2023
ISBN: 979-8-218-23845-2

Dedication

Josephine Collins (*Mama*), Yvonne Collins (*Sister*), Gregg Payne, and Carolyn Lewis-Stone – collectively, the wind beneath my wings.

Much appreciation to
Vincent Miller, James Edward Alexander, Crystal Hanton Johnson, William Thompson, Reginald Richardson, Jasmine Collins, Marlys Deen, Nicole Collins, Jessica Collins, and Clarence Collins, II.

CONTENTS

- Preface 6
- Introduction 8

1. Keys to the Kingdom (*Education*) 10
2. Honoring the Ancestors (*Traditions*) 28
3. The Importance of Financial Freedom *(Wealth)* 37
4. Reading is Fundamental (*Literacy*) 52
5. Living Longer (*Health*) 61
6. Black Families (*Responsibility*) 68
7. What's Love Got to Do with It? (*Relationships*) 74
8. What About God? (*Spirituality*) 82
9. If You Can Go to Jail (*Obstacles*) 86
10. Release the Fear (*Stress*) 95
11. About the Author 107

PREFACE

Imagine the incredible power of changing the direction of your life by delving deep into your history and using what you discover to shape your present. Would the rhythm of your steps change? Would the patterns of your thoughts transform? Could you truly see your life from a fresh perspective, all in the passionate pursuit of creating a life that goes beyond the ordinary, a life of greatness and victory? Would you have the courage to start this journey?

The potential for change becomes clear when we think about how learning from our past and applying it to our present can reshape our future. Each piece of our history holds hidden wisdom, and within that wisdom lies the power to reshape our course. Can we, by carefully examining each piece of our past, create a new picture that blends with our dreams, forming a life that stands out from the usual?

"10 Things Your Mama Should Have Told You" is more than just a book; it acts as a model, a plan that shapes the life we want to create. The connection between its teachings and our efforts urges us to rise to a higher purpose, to internalize its guidance, and to show its wisdom through our choices. To explore this path, we need to understand its message and integrate its wisdom into our very being, transforming ourselves into creators of our own future.

The symphony of an extraordinary life is a composition where the echoes of our past combine with the decisions we make today, creating a masterpiece of importance. Every action we take, every choice we make, adds to the potential for greatness. This is not just a theoretical journey; it's an exploration of our own depths, a moment where our past meets our future possibilities.

With the knowledge we gain from our past experiences, we find ourselves at a crossroads, holding the pen that writes our story. The echoes of our history mix with the urgency of the present, urging us to shape our destiny with purpose and boldness. Will you answer this call? Will you walk through the chapters of

10 Things Your Mama Should Have Told You, conducting a life that's exceptional, a life that's triumphant?

The inspiration behind *10 Things Your Mama Should Have Told You* emerged from dialogues with family, friends, peers, students, and their parents. Many aspects of African American life remain hidden until later years, leaving us feeling that we've missed out. This isn't a criticism of our parents, as they didn't intend to handicap us socially, emotionally, financially, or intellectually. It's likely that there were things they weren't aware of. These influential factors have contributed to an ongoing cycle of challenges.

The present moment beckons us to shatter the psychological chains of poverty and ignorance that have been historically associated with individuals of African descent. It's time to rectify past misfortunes and misguided steps, and to set forth on a path of enlightenment and achievement. Certainly, racism plays a role in these struggles, yet we must find ways to navigate around, though, and beyond its barriers. The time has come to eliminate any obstacles blocking our progress and forge ahead.

Just as our ancestors aspired for prosperity, good health, and education, there's no reason we should expect or settle for anything less. We have more than 150 years of history to guide us. The only directions worth following are those leading us forward and upward. And even in the face of challenges, remember what doesn't defeat us only makes us stronger.

INTRODUCTION

As a young child, I couldn't fathom why injustices persisted despite our nation learning about the atrocities inflicted on people of African descent. The brutal and inhumane slave trade, where African people were transported to the Americas to toil without pay, left a lasting scar. This horrific practice spanned the 16th to 19th centuries, contributing to the oppression of African Americans while bolstering the wealth of white Americans.

The legacy of slavery meant African Americans were denied generational wealth while their white counterparts flourished. This financial disparity manifested in society, dividing individuals into "haves" and "have nots." The impacts of slavery still resonate today, affecting various aspects of our lives.

History witnessed events that hindered the progress of African Americans. Families were torn apart, housing opportunities were segregated, job opportunities were scarce, and education was unequal. Colleges denied entry to black students, churches were bombed, medical care was limited, and police brutality and the prison system wreaked havoc on families. These injustices have stagnated lives.

Discrimination and racial bias have consistently suppressed black individuals. Proof of this bias is evident in historical events and the omission of crucial information. From the American Civil War and Reconstruction to the Tulsa Race Riots, Hurricane Katrina, and the Black Lives Matter movement, systemic challenges have hindered African American progress.

Reconstruction, following the Civil War, aimed to reunite the nation, reshape the South, and secure full civil rights for African Americans in the 20th century. Though seen as a positive initiative, some argue it ultimately failed, contributing to ongoing oppression and racial violence.

The landmark Supreme Court case, Brown vs. Board of Education, is integral to

American history. The struggle to end school segregation in 1954 still profoundly affects people of African descent. The case, brought forth by Oliver Brown and others, challenged the constitutionality of segregation policies. Thurgood Marshall's successful argument led the court to conclude that separate facilities were inherently unequal

Despite its significance, Brown vs. Board of Education is often inadequately taught, preventing young African Americans from comprehending its historical importance. Similarly, events like the Tulsa Race Riot, where prosperous African American communities were destroyed, have lasting consequences. Hurricane Katrina in 2005 showcased the plight of the neglected and poor, disproportionately impacting African Americans. Thousands were stranded due to lack of money or transportation, resulting in tragic loss of life and livelihoods. This disaster highlighted the racial and economic disparities in our society.

In analyzing these historical events, we uncover lessons learned and contemplate their implications for our lives. The challenges of the past shape our present and future. To overcome them, we must educate ourselves, break free from fear and ignorance, and forge a path towards prosperity.

Our life spans are limited, and good health is crucial. We must equip ourselves and future generations with the tools needed for prosperity. We've distanced ourselves from the achievements of our ancestors, but we can regain our footing by arming ourselves with knowledge and adapting to our changing world and economy.

As we navigate a complex world, it's clear that education and equality are key. Breaking free from the chains of history and striving for a better future is our responsibility.

Chapter 1

Keys to the Kingdom

(Education)

"Knowledge is power and as such holds every key to every chain and shackle. It always did, it always will."
Ossie Davis

The role of education as an equalizer can be seen in different social classes within our society. It impacts the lives of those from affluent backgrounds to the middle class and even the lower class. Education has a significant impact on our lives, from financial difficulties to health problems and living conditions. Those with less education often face more challenges and lower quality of life.

Passing down the importance of education from one generation to the next is crucial. Families who value education and pass it on strategically tend to achieve more success and satisfaction. Education acts as a precious heirloom, passed down through generations. Enslaved Africans recognized the value of education as a prized gift. Education has held a special place in our history, with many Black individuals seeking access to knowledge and power.

Education is one of our sacred heirlooms that can be guaranteed and passed down from one generation to the next generation. Education is a precious gift all must be opened to receiving. Enslaved Africans identified obtaining an education as one of the most esteemed and precious gifts.

Education has been honorably positioned at the pinnacle of a remarkable journey. According to Heather Andrea Williams in her book *African American Education in Slavery and Freedom (2003)*, "Blacks wanted access to reading and writing as a way to attain the very information and power that whites strove to withhold from them." Many families believed that the attainment of a quality education was key to success.

Unlike some of the information learned in elementary and secondary school, our history did not begin with slavery. In Africa, there were kingdoms and city-states, each with its own language and culture. The people of West Africa had rich and diverse histories and cultures centuries before Europeans arrived. The empire of Songhai and the kingdoms of Mali, Benin, and Kongo were large and powerful with monarchs heading complex political structures governing hundreds of thousands of people (*Jim Crow Museum, 2022*). There were kings, pharaohs, and queens who shaped our ancestor's lives.

Our history goes beyond slavery, with Africans contributing to technological advancements and shaping civilizations. African societies had their own languages, cultures, and powerful rulers. African kings, queens, and leaders played significant roles. Some of these notable kings in Africa included Akhenaten - a Pharaoh of Egypt, Menelik, the first Emperor of Ethiopia; Shaka Zula the founder of the Zulu Empire; Oba Oduduwa, divine kingdom of Yoruba; and Mansa Mata Marisa of the Mali Empire, one of the richest kingdoms of Africa.

Among the distinguish queens were Amina, the Queen of Zaira Nigeria, and Nzinga Queen of Ndongo and Matamba. Nzinga fought successfully to keep the colonizers from Portuguese at bay. In addition, there were Kandake, the Empress of Ethiopia: Makeda, the queen of Sheba, Ethiopia; Nefertiti, the Queen of Ancient Kemet, Egypt, and Yaa Asantewa, Ashanti Kingdom, Ghana.

Most descendants to the crown had the crown passed down to them. They trained expeditiously for the role of future king or queen. They were warriors who fought to protect their country and people. They are noteworthy because they made a major difference in prolonging our existence and speaking to our gifts and strengths.

Art, reading, and technology flourished, and Africans were especially skilled in medicine, mathematics, and astronomy. In addition to domestic goods, they made fine luxury items in bronze, ivory, gold, and terracotta for both local use and trade. They contributed to our world before they were enslaved.

There were many narratives written during the 1840's and onwards. The writers of those narratives were among the most admirable black Americans of their time. They struggled against the indignities and oppressions of slavery, and some even successfully escaped from bondage. After their escape, they often devoted themselves to enlightening and liberating others.

What was also noteworthy was their desire to master the art of reading and writing. And, ultimately, their pursuit of some form of an education. Education played a key role for many African American figures like Frederick Douglass, and Booker T. Washington. They recognized the importance of reading and learning, overcoming challenges to pursue knowledge.

Frederick Douglass' *Narrative of the Life of Frederick Douglass, An American Slave* was written in 1845. Douglass recognized at an early age the connection between reading and writing, with respect and success. Douglass would often trick young white boys into teaching him to read by pretending that he could. After he would fumble on pronunciations, they would correct him all the while laughing at Douglass' ignorance. The game was played so frequently that Douglass eventually increased his ability to recognize words and infer their meanings. And before long he was reading. Even though reading was against the law for slaves, Douglass' indomitable spirit was unwavering.

Douglass would read by candlelight. He would find discarded newspapers in the street and practice recitation in front of his peers. Eventually he would read the entire bible. This practice would also serve to provide him with his first lesson in public speaking. He worked diligently to enunciate every syllable. Many great orators have shared that they too utilized this same approach - reading the bible or even Shakespeare aloud to improve their diction. Douglass desired a better life as a free man and worked to ensure that when that day came, he would be ready.

Booker T. Washington was born in 1856. After the Civil War, his family moved to Malden, West Virginia. He worked in the salt and coalmines by day and attended school by night. In 1872, driven by the desire for an education, he made his way to the Hampton Normal and Agricultural Institute nearly 300 miles away by walking and hitchhiking. Later, he formed the Tuskegee Institute for higher learning. A year after his speech entitled The Atlanta Compromise, Harvard University made Washington an honorary Master of Arts. In 1901 Dartmouth College conferred the LL. D – Doctor of Literary Letters upon him.

At the onset of reconstruction, many ex-slaves held onto the belief that in order to break free from the psychological chains of their past lives, they must receive an education. Sometimes financial situations would not allow every child in a family to attend school. Some were remanded to the fields from sunrise to sunset, while others were allowed to attend school. This notion did not prevent them from teaching each other.

Noted scholar Dr. W.E.B. DuBois, though not born into slavery was born in 1868. He began his studies at Fisk University at the age of 17. In 1888, after graduation from Fisk University he attended Harvard University. He graduated two years later in a class of 300. He earned his master's degree after one year of work and had completed most of his doctoral dissertation by the end of the second year. His dissertation *The Suppression of the African Slave Trade to the United States of America, 1638-1870,* was published in 1896, which was the same year he was awarded his doctorate. He is also the author of *The Souls of Black Folk*.

Douglass, Washington, and DuBois are three stellar examples of one utilizing education to enhance the quality of their lives - despite obstacles imposed on their race. Their journey did not end after they received their degrees - they felt obligated to share their knowledge and encourage others to travel their paths. Even after their successes, it should be noted that people of African descent were not always afforded the opportunity to attend school.

African Americans have historically faced systemic barriers to education, including segregation, and limited access to quality schooling. Education serves as a means to overcome these historical inequities and bridge the gap in educational opportunities. It allows African Americans to assert their right to education and work towards achieving equal access and success.

In today's world, educational inequities still exist, especially in urban and rural areas. Poor communities often have lower standards and fewer resources in schools. Education empowers individuals with knowledge and skills, enabling them to navigate society, make informed decisions, and advocate for change.

Education empowers individuals with knowledge, skills, and critical thinking abilities. It enables African Americans to develop their intellectual capabilities, broaden their horizons, and cultivate a sense of self-worth and self-determination. Education equips individuals with the tools needed to navigate society, make informed decisions, and advocate for themselves and their communities.

The achievement gap between black and white students is influenced by class and economic factors. While financial challenges can widen this gap, knowledge and power can elevate aspirations. Efforts are needed to review and improve education quality, especially in underfunded schools.

Urban schools are further behind in terms of preparing their students for higher education. Granted, many underfunded schools are able to achieve great results with their students because of the leadership of the schools, but that is the exception and not the rule. There must be a concerted effort to review the quality of education in our communities. We need to understand the curriculum that is being taught and fight for updates and revisions when necessary.

Today there are states working to remove pertinent information from the curriculum. They are specifically advocating for removal of information about black history. This is where parents have to step in and fight. Also, parents are the first teacher in a child's life. Therefore, if a school does not teach the curriculum the parents must equip themselves with the know ledge to do so.

Education is crucial in addressing racial disparities and promoting equity. African American studies, literature, and cultural education are essential to preserve and celebrate heritage. Visionary educators in New York City, like Dr. Adelaide L. Sanford, Lorraine Monroe, and Geoffrey Canada have made strides in raising educational standards.

Dr. Adelaide L. Sanford was a teacher, assistant principal, and principal in Brooklyn, New York. She also taught education courses at Baruch College and

Fordham University. In 1986 she became Member-at-Large for the Board of Regents of the State of New York. In 2001 she was elected as Vice Chancellor of the Board of Regents.

Throughout her career, Dr. Sanford has been an advocate for equitable education, focusing on issues such as school desegregation, improving educational outcomes for minority students, and promoting inclusive curricula. She has been recognized for her dedication to education and her efforts to address systemic inequalities within the educational system.

Dr. Lorraine Monroe was an influential educator and the founder of the Frederick Douglass Academy (FDA), a highly regarded public school in New York City. The Frederick Douglass Academy is known for its rigorous academic curriculum, strong emphasis on college preparation, and commitment to empowering students, particularly young men of color, to achieve their full potential.

Lorraine Monroe's visionary approach to education focused on providing a nurturing and challenging learning environment for students who may have faced barriers to success. She believed in the transformative power of education and aimed to provide students with the tools and support they needed to excel academically and beyond.

Under her leadership, the Frederick Douglass Academy gained a reputation for its high graduation rates, college acceptance rates, and success in preparing students for higher education. Lorraine Monroe's work at the academy and her dedication to educational equity have left a lasting impact on the lives of countless students.

Geoffrey Canada is an educational advocate and the founder of the Harlem Children's Zone (HCZ), a comprehensive community-based organization aimed at providing educational, social, and health services to children and families in Harlem, New York City. The HCZ is known for its holistic approach to addressing the challenges faced by children growing up in underserved neighborhoods.

Canada's vision for the Harlem Children's Zone was to create a "cradle-to-college" pipeline of support for children, ensuring they receive quality education, family support, and access to various resources from early childhood through college. The HCZ offers a range of programs, including early childhood education, after-school programs, family support services, and college preparation initiatives.

Geoffrey Canada's work with the Harlem Children's Zone has garnered national attention and praise for its innovative approach to tackling issues related to poverty, education, and community development. He has been a prominent advocate for educational reform and has shared his insights and strategies with policymakers and educators around the country.

Sanford, Monroe, and Canada are notable for their efforts to transform education in New York City, but it is still the responsibility of our communities to ensure that our children receive the best education possible. Sometimes financial situations can put us in precarious situations where the only school we can attend or send our child to is the one in the neighborhood. Sometimes the schools are decent, and they will offer a quality program that prepares them for college. But if you're like a good number of families living in urban and rural settings, the schools are not the best. So, what do you do?

Hopefully you have heard the adage: it's not where you start but where you finish. This motto encourages us to seek the best in all situations. If your child has to attend a neighborhood school, ensure that they take advantage of everything possible during their tenure in school. Seek out programs that will encourage academic excellence. Motivate them to join clubs. Emphasize that they work to maintain a decent grade point average – "B" or 85% and above. Attend their parent teacher conferences throughout their educational career. Do not stop once they enter high school. Stay involved in your child's life throughout their school career. You are required to be there until they graduate college.

If your child maintains stellar grades and continues to work and study throughout high school and college, they will be able to change their economic station in life. If they drop out of school, they are establishing a blueprint for a tumultuous life. Additionally, they are also setting up any progeny that they may later bring into the world for failure. A deficit will be established and will place them behind in the game and create an unnecessary handicap. It is akin to cutting off one of their feet and then feigning surprise when they come in last place during an important race.

Education is not only beneficial for individuals, but also for the collective empowerment and transformation of African American communities. Educated individuals can serve as role models, mentors, and advocates, helping to uplift their communities and effect positive change. Education fosters community engagement, critical thinking, and problem-solving skills necessary for addressing social, economic, and political challenges.

Research states, segregated schools receive inequitable resources for their students. Segregated schools historically have low-performing teachers. Yet somehow in spite of it all some school's rise and inspire a nation to come together and continue to rise. The Paul Laurence Dunbar High School was such a school.

In 1916, the Paul Laurence Dunbar High School was the most prestigious high school for Blacks in the country. The Dunbar School was a college preparatory school where students followed a classical curriculum. Dunbar High was an academically elite public school, despite being racially segregated by law and existing at the mercy of racist congressmen who held the school's purse strings.

The Jim Crow laws prevented many highly qualified Blacks from obtaining work in their studied profession, and as such, they worked in the Black public school system and upheld high expectations for the students. Dunbar developed the reputation of being a high-performing high school, and families were eager to enroll their children in the school, even if they had to relocate to DC. According to Bernard (2012), *"in 1917, Dunbar had 146 graduating seniors, which was far more than any other black high school in the country. Fifty-nine of its graduates that year continued on to college, while fifty-seven went to normal schools."* "Normal schools" were institutions of higher learning that trained students to become teachers.

The students were challenged and motivated to achieve and surpassed their white counterparts on a national assessment. Dismayed, the superintendent switched out the high performing black teachers with lower performing white teachers. He reassigned the black superintendent and principal.

The Paul Laurence Dunbar High School would continue to ensure high standards and edification of its pupils despite the disparities in pay for teachers and administrators, facilities, resources, and support. The school would continue to attract the best Black educators and leaders in spite of systems created to thwart their employment.

Based on the demographics posted on its current website, as well as the District of Columbia Public School (DCPS) website, the Paul Laurence Dunbar High School continues to serve the children of Washington DC, where its student population remains segregated (*Dunbar Website, 2017*). An effort to integrate schools became a problem for schools across the nation as more public schools opened and remained segregated and unequal.

There are countless examples of our ancestors fighting for equity at the table of education. Many died for their struggles and beliefs for our ultimate seat at the table of higher education. Our desire and commitment to receive the best education should never be taken for granted. It is our birthright. Our success is payment in full for the countless struggles fought by our ancestors.

It's important to remember that education is a gift earned through the sacrifices of ancestors. Seeking knowledge should be innate and celebrated. Education benefits not only individuals but also the collective community by fostering critical thinking, problem-solving, and positive change.

There is a belief that history details the past and has nothing to do with either the present or the future. This belief is shallow and does not serve to honor the legacies and contributions of so many who believed in our futures. Societal forces have been allowed to inform us of whom we are, while we, in essence have turned our backs on the contributions of so many daring individuals.

Somehow, we have been led to believe that if we investigate and celebrate our historical contributions that we are being - afro-centric - as if being afro-centric is a negative concept. Being black or African centered is currently missing in the majority of our homes today. We have worked so hard to be accepted at the table of equality but forgetting our ancestor's work.

When we investigate and learn our history, that knowledge informs everything we do. We begin to feel an obligation to help and inform others and this encourages them to be the absolute best they can be. It becomes infectious. There was a time in reconstruction where people of African descent did not want to diminish African culture but felt compelled to be accepted as Americans. We did not recognize the duality of our consciousness. Part of the problem involved being identified as anything that was represented as being white in America.

There was much disdain for the traditions that were associated with being an American. Our wounds were still open, and we chose not to assimilate into mainstream society. Yet, mainstream society is the majority society. We should maintain what is American, while celebrating what is African. We share two consciousnesses. And too often this duality comes across as burdensome, yet it is our inherited right.

Our present generation is held ever tighter by stronger grips of racism. Racism today is more covert, or undercover, than ever before. This cluelessness has no way of recognizing the signs even when they are clearly spelled out. Too many believe that all of the work has been done. They believe our race has been redeemed and accepted by mainstream society. This philosophy only serves to create a generation of ignorant and uninformed people who will serve no purpose other than setting the race back 100 years. This notion also supports the contention that we should remain in the underbelly of American society, instead of showcasing and celebrating our contributions to the wonderful landscape of this country.

We must rewrite history books with a pride that details the vast contributions of our ancestors. But until that time, you must seek out our history and become knowledgeable about on whose shoulders we stand. If the parent is clear – their children will be clearer. You must also take advantage of all educational opportunities especially the arts.

Arts Education

Arts education holds immense value, enriching both individuals and society as a whole. Here are several significant benefits of integrating arts into education:

1. **Enhanced Creativity and Innovation**: Arts education fosters creativity and encourages individuals to think outside the box. It cultivates innovative thinking and problem-solving skills, which are essential for success in various fields.

2. **Improved Academic Performance**: Studies show that students engaged in arts education often perform better academically. Arts help develop critical thinking, analytical skills, and the ability to interpret and synthesize information.

3. **Cultural Understanding and Appreciation**: Arts expose students to diverse cultures, traditions, and historical periods. This cultivates an understanding and appreciation of different perspectives, promoting tolerance and empathy.

4. **Enhanced Communication Skills**: Arts education, including drama, music, and visual arts, improves communication skills, including verbal and non-verbal expression. Students learn to articulate thoughts, emotions, and ideas effectively.

5. **Confidence and Self-Expression**: Participating in the arts boosts self-esteem and self-confidence. It provides a platform for students to express themselves authentically and gain a sense of accomplishment, essential for personal growth.

6. **Teamwork and Collaboration**: Many art forms involve group projects and performances, promoting collaboration and teamwork. Students learn to work together, respect others' ideas, and appreciate the collective effort.

7. **Preservation of Culture and Heritage:** Arts education plays a vital role in preserving cultural heritage and traditions. It ensures that artistic traditions are passed down from generation to generation, maintaining a rich and diverse cultural tapestry.

An education integrated with the arts adds immense value to the learning experience, promoting creativity, critical thinking, cultural understanding, and personal development. It prepares individuals for success in various aspects of life, fostering a society enriched with creativity, empathy, and appreciation for the arts.

Imagine that your child's tenure in school is akin to depositing money in the bank. The deposit earns interests at a high rate. Thereby providing your child, upon withdrawal, with myriad tools to ensure their success in life. Their work and contributions will be equated with a fulfilling life that is replete with personal and financial successes. In this manner we will ensure that we do not need the assistance of affirmative action. We will be able to stand and compete regardless of our socio-economic standings.

Parents usually support their children during grades Pre-K through 5. By the time the child reaches junior high school, most parents believe they have to give their child some space to assert independence. They stop attending PTA meetings, and they rarely check on their child's academic standing until parent-teacher conferences. They stop checking homework assignments, and some parents even ignore low attendance reports. These disconnects only serve to further handicap an already at-risk child.

While most cities do provide services for children who are at-risk, there are no national systems in place to check the merit of such programs. As such, the children can end up learning nothing. They will continue to spiral downward into the will not graduate high school category, or they become a discipline problem in the classroom. Now you are faced with having to come to school to advocate on behalf of your suspended child. While your child is serving a suspension, they are missing out on lessons their peers are receiving. This factor also serves to move them further away from graduating high school on time. The probability of this child graduating high school becomes slim, while the prospect of college becomes a mere fantasy.

I am always saddened when I hear my students say, "I will be the first member of my family to graduate high school." Usually when a teen states this fact – the audience applauds. I always ponder the foundation of the family. We have more advances and educational opportunities, therefore in 2023, children should not be the first to graduate high school and attend college. Why are we not graduating from high school? Who lowered the bar? What happened to our honoring and respecting the prospects of an education? It is definitely not in our history to forsake our education. If our enslaved ancestors valued an education and died to receive one – who are we to assign it to a lower rung on our ladder to success?

Granted, there will be some individuals who are self-directed. Somehow, they get it, and work at keeping it. This will amount to about 1 out 4 – for a family with 4 children. Trust me, you will have to do the work with the remaining 3 children. Whatever the approach, children always need guidance. High expectations must be a regular part of your family's discussions. There are too many obstacles awaiting young people of color. Acceptance into college is more than a lofty goal for our children; it is part of their obligation to their ancestors and themselves.

The 12 years spent in secondary school will pass whether students work hard or not. It is a known fact that individuals who studied in school and read books were more successful spiritually and financially than those who did not. We should always aim for intelligence and knowledge. Refuse to accept less. Encourage yourself and your children to become life-long learners. If the parents make education important in their homes and live by that example, their children will naturally follow suit. If you dropped out of high school, you must discuss this with your children. Explain why and emphasize how you want more for them. Plan to return and earn a GED, vocational certification, and then a college degree. It is never too late.

Maintain high expectations for yourself and your children. This notion will encourage everyone to move towards educational excellence. As you continue your journey with your child, understand that you are growing as well. You are creating and designing your life and the lives of your future progeny. If you allow your children to waste time, understand that they will not be able to recoup it. It is gone forever. On the other hand, if you carefully carve out your children's journey, they will begin to understand the value of life and how they should never take a moment for granted.

Education is a gift granted to people of African descent through the blood, sweat, tears and untimely death of too many who came before us. Our ancestor's sacrifices should never be taken for granted or forgotten. Seeking edification for your children's mind and spirit should be as innate as teaching them to walk.

Education is beneficial for the collective empowerment and transformation of African American communities. Educated individuals can serve as role models, mentors, and advocates, helping to uplift their communities and effect positive change. Education fosters community engagement, critical thinking, and problem-solving skills necessary for addressing social, economic, and political challenges.

Current challenges include the gender gap in college enrollment and graduation rates among African American men. Females already outnumber males at most colleges, but the gap is especially large among black students. Nationally, barely a quarter of the 1.9 million black men between 18 and 24 – prime college-going years – were in college in 2006, according to the American Council on Education's report on minorities in higher education. By comparison, 35 percent of black women in the same age group and 36 percent of all 18- to 24-year-olds were enrolled in higher education.

The graduation rate of black males is lower than that of any other group. Only 35 percent of the black men who entered N.C.A.A. Division I colleges in 2022 for example, graduated within six years, compared with 59 percent of white men, 46 percent of Hispanic men, 41 percent of American Indian men and 45 percent of black women who entered the same year.

Researchers say the obstacles keeping black men from earning college degrees include poor education before college, the low expectations that teachers and others have for them, a lack of black men as role models, their dropout rate from high school and their own low aspirations. While most of these problems are common to disadvantaged minority students regardless of sex, black men have the special burden of being pigeonholed early in a way that black females are not. This was among the findings of the African American Male Initiative, a program set up by the University System of Georgia to research and remove the obstacles to college enrollment and graduation for black men.

If you have not completed a high school education, how do you expect to impart the knowledge that is necessary for your child's growth? If you have not completed college how do you expect to sustain an income to assist supporting your family? If you did not complete high school – you must return and bring closure to that element of your life. Enroll in college if you have the opportunity and graduate. Set multiple goals and work to realize them. Set an example for yourself and any current or projected children.

It is important to recognize that the significance of education extends beyond the individual level for African Americans. Education serves as a catalyst for personal growth, societal progress, and the pursuit of social justice. By embracing the power of education, African Americans can work towards breaking down barriers, fostering equity, and creating a more inclusive and just society. By achieving higher levels of education, African Americans can demonstrate their intellectual capabilities and contribute to society in meaningful ways, while also challenging negative stereotypes and biases.

Summary
- This chapter discusses the role of education as an equalizer across social classes, emphasizing its impact on financial difficulties, health, and living conditions.
- It underscores the importance of passing down the value of education through generations and highlights the historical significance of education in African American communities.
- The chapter also showcases the achievements of notable African American figures such as Frederick Douglass, Booker T. Washington, and W.E.B. DuBois in their pursuit of education despite challenges.
- It discusses the contributions of African societies to history, and the importance of education in addressing racial disparities and promoting equity today.

- It concludes with the reminder that education is a gift earned through the sacrifices of ancestors, and its benefits extend to both individuals and the collective community.

Chapter 2
Honoring the Ancestors
(Traditions)

"Bringing the gifts that my ancestors gave
I am the hope and the dream of the slave.
I Rise"
Dr. Maya Angelou

Understanding one's origins should evoke a rightful sense of pride. In the context of this nation, African Americans have endured significant atrocities that have shaped lives, history, and significance. From the brutal transatlantic journey to ongoing discrimination, the experiences of descendants of Africa have been unique and marked by psychological manipulation and violence

These struggles have had lasting effects on subsequent generations, impacting self-esteem, financial opportunities, and cultural identity. Historical events like Jim Crow laws, segregation, and the civil rights movement underscore the inequalities faced. Acts of violence against African American communities, church bombings, and murders have disrupted progress, yet the spirit endures.

We have studied the laws of Jim Crow, segregation, and on the surface - the civil rights movement in school. We are constantly reminded of inequities as we were plunged into accepting lower standards in our schools, suffered through the atrocities of lynching, and settled into communities where all hope was lost. Fear and despair were deeply etched in our psyche but did not impede our progress.

There are many examples in history that denotes how African Americans have been persecuted. Churches were bombed, and children were murdered. Our wealth was stolen. Our sense of family, culture, and racial pride was destroyed. Our leaders were assassinated. They were some of the greatest minds this country has ever produced. Yet they were taken removed too soon. But we are still here.

We have an unwritten obligation to our ancestors to honor their sacrifices. Many marched, delivered speeches, boycotted, integrated, went to jail, and gave their lives to ensure that we would understand our greatness – and we should not ever forget that. We must learn our history. We must teach our children their history. We must expose our progeny to the greatness of our race, so they understand on whose shoulders they stand.

We are here because we stand on the shoulders of those who came before us. Their lives continue to impact our lives today. It is important to know who they were, what they did, and why we must always celebrate their contributions. Their stories are road maps for our journey and make apparent our majestic potential. We must instill in ourselves and our children a sense of racial pride.

Honoring our ancestors' sacrifices obliges us to learn their stories and convey their greatness to future generations. We're indebted to their legacy, standing on their shoulders. Influential figures like Dr. Martin Luther King, Jr., Paul Robeson, Harriet Tubman, Marcus Garvey, Hattie McDaniel, Ruby Dee, Muhammad Ali, Toussaint L'Ouverture, and Nelson Mandela serve as exemplars of resilience and activism.

Dr. Martin Luther King, Jr. was born on January 15, 1929 and entered Morehouse College at the age of 15. After graduation, he became a minister. His involvement was instrumental in CORE (Congress of Racial Equality), SNCC (Student Nonviolent Coordinating Committee), and SCLC (Southern Christian Leadership Conference). In 1963 he organized a campaign to stop segregation in Birmingham, Alabama. He demanded desegregation of lunch counters, restrooms, and drinking fountains. On December 4, 1964, Dr. King was awarded the Nobel Peace Prize. He was also instrumental in the drafting of the Civil Rights Act, which ended some segregation, and the Voting Rights Act. He was the keynote speaker at the March on Washington in 1968.

I have always admired Dr. King. My earliest memory is in 1968. I remember being in class when it was announced that he had been assassinated. We were told to put our heads down on our desk and say a prayer for the family of this great man. Many teachers cried. At the time, I did not fully understand the ramifications of his death. Later I would journey to the library and read everything I could about his life.

There are numerous books written on the life of Dr. King. He is someone everyone should have knowledge of. What did he stand for? What was he willing to do to get what he wanted? What about his family and friends? Why non-violence? Why was he murdered in 1968? What does his journey mean for Blacks? Dr. King advocated for the rights of all people. And he had "a dream that one day we would not be judge by the color of our skin, but by the content of our character." In 2008, we saw the fruits of his labor made manifest in the election of Barack Obama our first black president of the United States of America.

Paul Robeson was born in 1898. He was a scholar, athlete, and actor. He also possessed one of the finest baritones voices this country had ever heard. Additionally, he was an activist who fought for the rights of his people. He attended Rutgers University where he became a member of Phi Beta Kappa, a national college honor society. He graduated Valedictorian of his class. He later attended Columbia University's Law School where he earned his law degree in two years.

Robeson became interested in acting. He performed the role of Joe in the musical, Showboat, on Broadway. He made stage history in 1930, in London, with his magnificent portrayal of Shakespeare's Othello. He also performed in Eugene O'Neill's All God's Chillun Got Wings, and The Emperor Jones, and Porgy and Bess. He received critical acclaim. He paved the way for actors Sidney Poiter, Denzel Washington, Jeffrey Wright, Samuel L. Jackson and many others.

By the 1930's Robeson's interests shifted towards politics and he began his work towards racial justice. This journey led him to become associated with the Communist party - which led to him being blacklisted and unable to secure work as an actor or singer. His passport was revoked in 1950 preventing him from traveling outside of the country. Robeson once said, "As I went out into life, one thing loomed above all else: I was my father's son, a former slave, a Negro in America. That was the challenge." He died in 1976.

Harriet Tubman was born into slavery in 1821. She recognized early that slavery was inhumane. She eventually escaped in 1849 and spent the next sixteen years trying to free others. She joined the Underground Railroad where she freed more than 300 slaves.

During the Civil War she worked as a nurse, scout, and spy for the Union Army. She also led a raid that freed over 750 slaves. She was nicknamed Moses for her perseverance in leading her people to the promise land – freedom. She died at the age of 92. There is a film entitled Harriet (2019) that depicts Harriet's escape from slavery, and how she freed hundreds of slaves. It is a must watch.

Marcus Garvey was born in Jamaica in 1887. He moved to London after being fired from his job for aiding in the organization of a strike. While in Europe, he attended the University of London. When he returned to Jamaica, he organized the Universal Negro Improvement Association (UNIA) with the sole purpose of making Africa "the defender of Negroes the world over." He published the Negro World magazine and planned to organize 400 million black people of the world into a free republic of Africa. He even bought a steamship to transport individuals back to Africa.

In 1920 he staged a month-long convention in Harlem that attracted thousands from all over the world. He raised more than $10 million dollars. Unfortunately, his dreams were never realized as he was charged and convicted of mail fraud and was eventually deported to Jamaica after serving two of a five - year jail sentence. He later returned to London where he died in 1940.

Hattie McDaniel was one of the early faces in black and white movies-before cable and video rentals. Ms. Daniels was the first African American actress to win an Academy Award in 1939 for the film Gone with the Wind. She was also the first Black women to sing on radio in the United States. Her work as an actress paved the way for others. While she consistently played the role of maids or mammy's, Hattie attempted to inject pride in her work on-screen and in her private life. She was quoted as saying "I'd rather play a maid than be a maid." Because of her triumphant spirit actresses today have a broader selection of roles to choose from in the entertainment industry.

Ruby Dee was one of the actresses who deviated from the roles frequented by Hattie McDaniel. In my earlier years, I wanted to be an actor. Throughout school and part of my college education I performed in the theatre. My role models were slim, but I always appreciated the body of work exemplified by Ms. Dee.

Growing up in the seventies, there were minimum role models for young black girls aspiring to a life in the theatre. But there was always Ruby Dee in film after film. From her roles in *A Raisin in the Sun, St. Louis Blues, Do the Right Thing, Buck and the Preacher,* and *American Gangster* among many, she set the standard for excellence in acting. Ms. Dee's quiet presence served as an inspiration for many careers. When she was nominated for an Academy Award for her small role in *American Gangster* everyone was elated. But it was her work as an activist, along with her husband, Ossie Davis, that defined the blueprint for many lives.

I had the pleasure of meeting Ms. Dee and forging a relationship. I was honored when after replying to my adoration for her she said to "No, Evelyn, I am proud of you and the work you are doing in the school in theatre. It is an honor to meet you." I am still smiling.

Muhammad Ali was born in 1946. He won the gold medal in the 1960's Olympics. In 1964 he defeated Sonny Liston to become heavyweight champion of the world. In 1966, at the peak of his boxing career, Ali held fast to his convictions by refusing to participate in the war in Vietnam. He believed it was contradictory to kill people who had not threatened his life in the United States. He stated, "I don't recall no Viet Cong ever calling me a nigger. My fight is right here in this country." Ali was sentenced to a jail term in 1967 for his refusal to be drafted. He was stripped of his heavy weight title. Yet he remained proud of his commitments. He remained free during his conviction was on appeal. In 1971 his appeal reached the Supreme Court, and this conviction was reversed.

Muhammad Ali should serve as a role model because of his steadfast commitment to his beliefs and dedication to his convictions. He was a legendary boxer and humanitarian, made significant contributions that extended far beyond the boxing ring. With his unmatched charisma, unwavering self-belief, and unapologetic stance against racial injustice and the Vietnam War, Ali became an icon of social activism. He fearlessly used his platform to advocate for civil rights and equality, inspiring millions worldwide. Ali's refusal to be drafted into the military, sacrificing his prime boxing years, showcased his unwavering principles. His magnetic personality and powerful words left an indelible impact, proving that one person's voice and actions can drive meaningful change and leave a lasting legacy for generations to come. **Many regards him as the greatest boxer of all time.**

Toussaint L'Ouverture - I discovered Toussaint while in preproduction for Ntozake Shange's choreopoem "for colored girls who have considered suicide/when the rainbow is enuf, at the University of Michigan. As a director of theatre, it is important to understand your subject matter and all of the names and references detailed in the play. Shange used Toussaint as part of the Lady in Brown's journey. "Toussaint wasn't afraid of anyone and he was going to free the slaves in Haiti." Toussaint was a Haitian general and a leader in the Haitian Revolution. He fought the French for the Haitian's independence. Toussaint is highly regarded for his tenacity and commitment to advocating for the rights of people of African descent in Haiti.

Nelson Mandela remains one of my all-time heroes for his work in ending apartheid in South Africa. Mandela served as the first president of South Africa. I can still remember how ecstatic I was when he was freed from prison in South Africa in 1992. My siblings and I were equally ecstatic to be a part of the celebration at Tiger Stadium in Detroit. Every seat in the stadium was filled. I admired Mandela's unending courage in the face of adversity. And I respect his commitment to South Africans in working tirelessly to end apartheid, even if it meant he would sacrifice 27 years of his life in prison. His story is worth investigating and honoring.

Dr. King's peaceful advocacy, Robeson's multifaceted accomplishments, Tubman's courage in freedom-fighting, Garvey's Pan-African movement, McDaniel's defiance in the face of stereotypes, Dee's acting and activism, Ali's principled stance, L'Ouverture's fight for Haitian independence, and Mandela's triumph over apartheid all resonate. Their stories provide roadmaps for progress, illuminating our potential. Through embracing racial pride, we continue their work. These trailblazers shaped education, challenged norms, and acted as beacons of change. Their stories underscore the significance of nonviolence, equality, and justice.

There are many African Americans who contributed to the shaping of our lives. To list and detail all of their contributions would fill multiple sets of books. We must embrace those who came before us so that we have a sense of where we are going. Our ancestor's lives were filled with both tragedy and victory. If we truly understood that we are standing on the shoulders of greatness we would not accept lowered standards. We should walk with pride knowing our ancestors overcame many tumultuous obstacles and were able to make major contributions to their communities and the world.

Their influence extends beyond their individual achievements. They inspire us to advocate for social justice, equality, and community-building. As we honor their memory, we actively contribute to the ongoing fight against racial disparities. Our progress is a testament to the strength of their legacy, proving that through resilience and unity, positive change is attainable.

Summary
- The chapter discusses the historical struggles and contributions of African Americans.
- It addresses the atrocities, discrimination, and challenges they faced, along with their significant achievements.
- The importance of understanding and honoring African American history, leaders like Dr. Martin Luther King Jr., Paul Robeson, Harriet Tubman, Marcus Garvey, Hattie McDaniel, Ruby Dee, Muhammad Ali, Toussaint L'Ouverture, and Nelson Mandela are highlighted.

- The chapter emphasizes the need to embrace their legacy, strive for progress, and continue the fight against racial inequalities through community-building and social justice efforts

Chapter 3
The Importance of Financial Freedom
(Wealth)

"Money makes the world go around."
Cabaret, Musical

Determining financial freedom involves assessing your current financial situation, defining your goals, and making informed decisions to achieve financial independence. Many people dream of various ways to generate wealth, such as winning the lottery or marrying into wealth. However, true financial freedom requires continuous education in financial literacy. Invest time in learning about personal finance, budgeting, investing, and money management through books, workshops, seminars, and reputable financial blogs.

Building wealth is achievable through various paths, including education, entrepreneurship, sports, arts, and professions. Regardless of the path, hard work is essential. The economic challenges faced by African Americans, including unemployment and home foreclosures, highlight the importance of financial knowledge and planning.

These are tough economic times for everyone, but especially for African Americans. The unemployment rate is more than 6.1% (2022), and home foreclosures continue to rise. Black homeowners experience foreclosure at a higher rate than white homeowners across the country. The question is why? Money can protect us from almost anything, but we tend not to have accumulated or inherited wealth.

Homeownership is crucial but often misunderstood. Understanding mortgages, interest rates, and responsible financial management is essential. Once high-interest debts are addressed and an emergency fund is established, focus on investing for the future. Consider retirement accounts, stock market investments, and real estate, seeking professional advice when necessary.

Disparities in financial habits and decisions contribute to racial economic challenges. Spending habits, credit scores, and investments play roles in financial outcomes. Education and wise financial choices can bridge these gaps.

Blacks make up only 13.2% of the U.S. population, yet account for 30% of the country's Scotch consumption. So impressed was Ford Motor Company with the

$46.7 billion that we spent on cars that the automaker commissioned Sean "P. Diddy" Combs, the entertainment and fashion mogul, to design a limited-edition Navigator replete with six plasma screens, three DVD players and a Sony PlayStation 2.

Spending as opposed to savings has affected many people. Some are afraid to answer their telephone due to the fear that it might be a bill collector. Yet, we continue to spend more money than we make. We spend most of our money on wants rather than needs. We also tend to purchase high-ticket items with credit cards. After purchasing the item with a credit card, we are often late making the minimum payment. This factor alone affects us in ways that we do not fully understand. Our record of how we spend and repay borrowed money is then reflected on our credit report.

African Americans must recognize the significance of credit reports. A positive credit report opens doors to low-interest loans and favorable terms. Co-signing loans, renting cars, or sharing financial responsibilities can have lasting impacts on credit. Developing a strong credit history, understanding FICO scores, and maintaining financial responsibility are critical.

Your credit report is something that should be checked every year to ensure that all of the information is correct. Knowing how creditors view you is important to your financial future. Only after you have amassed millions of dollars can you not worry about your credit report. The movers and shakers of the world keep a sharp and focused eye on all of their business matters, and your credit report is certainly a matter of business.

Develop a realistic budget that aligns with your financial goals. Track your expenses diligently to ensure that you are living within your means and making progress towards your objectives. Look for opportunities to reduce unnecessary spending and redirect those funds towards debt repayment, savings, or investments. Where do you desire to live? Who will extend you credit? What dealership will you purchase your car from? And more importantly, the interest rate assigned to your mortgage, car, and credit cards payments are all determined by your credit report.

Who sees your credit report? All financial lenders that you apply for credit from will see your credit report. They will take note of your credit rating and carefully analyze all of the information. If you possess a positive rating, you will be welcomed into the world of low or no interest on your loans. You will move into your dream house or drive that special car. Possess a negative rating and the doors will close faster than you can say I really like that.

There are many factors that can affect your credit rating. They will be discussed in no particular order, because they all have the ability to blast a hole in your credit worthiness. These acts include co-signing for a loan/lease; using your credit card to rent a car for a friend or family member; reserving a hotel room; paying for a trip with family or friends; sharing an apartment with a roommate and your name is solo on the lease; allowing someone to get their utilities (phone/electric/gas/water/cable) in your name; or any other good meaning deed that can leave you holding the bill. Family and friends prefer to be of assistance and don't plan on leaving you up the creek, but things happen. That's when you can faintly hear in the distance everyman for himself as the creditors take aim and come after you.

When you co-sign for anything you run the risk that the bill will not be paid. Otherwise, why would you need to co-sign? Therefore, see co-signing as a losing situation that can damage or end friendships or create an unnecessary strain on a relationship with a family member.

Can you blame your cousin for losing their job, or your friend for getting a divorce and incurring large alimony payments? How about your brother being laid off from his job? Any justification as to why they cannot make payment still means they cannot make the payment. Then you, accordingly, become responsible for the payments or risk the account going into collections - where it will stay on your credit report for seven long years. So, unless you have money that you can freely give people in their time of need do not co-sign or sign your name guaranteeing payment for another individual.

Why the hard nose approach? Simply put, all derogatory information stays on your credit report for seven years. Good credit references also stay on your report for seven years as well. So, isn't it better to compile positive credit references instead of negative ones? That's a no brainer.

A great number of people fail to learn the key elements to possessing an excellent credit report. I'm sure some of your mamas tried to explain the situation to you, or maybe they didn't, because they had a negative credit report themselves. Thus, they put the telephone in your brother's name, and the electricity in your sister's name, and the cable bill in your name. I could go on, but I think you get the point. As an adult it is your responsibility to discuss both money and credit with all of your children. Never be afraid to discuss money and the consequences of overspending or overextending with your children.

Steer away from purchasing items on credit. It is better to save money for larger purchases. If you can pay the bill off in 30-days, using a credit card is fine-if you cannot pay off the balance in 30-days, the purchase should wait. Another example of putting oneself at risk for a negative credit rating involves applying for credit cards when you don't have sufficient resources to pay the monthly bill. I know this tune firsthand, because I am guilty as charged.

When I graduated from the University of Michigan with my undergraduate degree, I was happy as a lark. My mother was proud, my siblings were proud, my neighbors were proud, and I was extremely proud. Completing college is no joke. It takes discipline, commitment, and hard work. At the completion of college, you are awarded your degree at commencement, and in the mail, a slew of applications for your first credit cards. Without even thinking about it, you alert your friends and family that you have arrived. MasterCard or American Express, have offered you a credit card and you don't even have a job.

I concluded that possessing a credit card was one of the perks of being a college graduate. My mother tried to tell me differently, but I failed to listen. Her first question was "how are you going to pay the bill without a job?" My college-educated response was "I'll be in Graduate School and can pay with my money from my fellowships. Besides my monthly bills will only be $20 a month." And we all know what happens after that.

I began to fervently use my card and paid the minimum payment of $20 a month. A year later the credit card company increased my credit limit. The company checked my record and noted my history of making payments on time and raised my credit limit. I told myself-I knew I could do it. Everything is good.

Oddly enough, I began to the view the money as free money. You know, money that is available for you to spend in whatever way you desire without real consequences. I began to charge things I really didn't need. I frequently took my friends out to dinner. I traveled and stayed in expensive hotels. I shopped, and shopped, and shopped. I kept a standing appointment at the beauty salon. And then the bills began to arrive.

To my amazement my monthly bills increased, but I could still pay the minimum. And I did. Then, before I knew it, I owed MasterCard, Visa, and American Express thousands of dollars. And I didn't have a job. I started to skip payments planning to double-up the next month - and that's never a good solution. The whistles were blowing, the red flags were waving, all in an attempt to alert me that I was heading for credit card collision.

In addition to my bachelor's degree, I also had a master's degree. I was ready to begin searching for a job. I sent out resumes and was quickly hired. Next, I had to find an apartment because I was no longer eligible to reside in student housing. The search began. I selected an apartment that had all of the amenities I had dreamed about only to be told that my application was denied due to negative information on my credit report.

I became incensed. I cited all of the excuses in the book. But I really failed to zoom in on the fact that my mama told me to leave credit cards alone until I was in a position to afford them. But I didn't listen. All of my late payments were reflected on my credit report. The months I decided to buy Christmas gifts instead of making my monthly payments was reflected on my credit report. All of my wild spending habits were reflected on my credit report. My credit limit compared to the available balance was a sure sign of an individual who had poor spending habits.

My less than stellar credit history revealed itself on my report for the next seven years. This is true even after I paid off the delinquent balances. My mama tried to tell me, all to no avail. Three years later I was ready to buy a house or condo. The bank was willing to assist me. They ordered a copy of my credit report to ascertain how well I had handled credit. They reviewed my credit report in addition to my FICO score. You are now thinking to yourself - what's a FICO score?

FICO Score
Your FICO Score ranges from 300 to 850 and takes into consideration your paying habits and use of previous and current credit accounts. It analyzes things like do you have any accounts in collections. Do you have any judgments pending? What is the ratio of your credit limits to your outstanding balances? Have you filed for bankruptcy or had a house go into foreclosure? Are any of your accounts past due? After analyzing the above information, a score is generated. It can range from high risk to low risk. This is the score creditors view when they determine whether you are eligible for credit, renting an apartment, or purchasing a car.

A score of 300 means no one will extend you credit, rent you a nice apartment, finance you a car, or provide you with a mortgage for that dream house. And, if you are granted credit with a high-risk score, the interest they will charge you to borrow the money will be extremely high. Let's review the example below:

You desire to borrow $165,000 for a mortgage for a lovely condo. Your FICO score is 529. All right, it's above 500 and some banks will approve your loan with a score above 500. But there's a catch. The lending agent informs you (maybe they don't) that the bank will charge you 9.0% interest on the loan. The bank can charge such an outrageous interest rate because you're in the high-risk arena. In essence, you will end up paying $270, 000 in interest on a 30-year fixed mortgage. The total amount due becomes $435,000 for a $165,000 loan. The same logic can be used when buying a car. You almost pay double the amount in interests for the use of the bank's money.

More than 75% of the applications for credit in the U.S. last year were decided with the help of a FICO score. If you fall in the 25% range, lenders may require additional information to help them evaluate your application for credit – factors may include your income or time at a job. So, if it's your first job - that may not be such a positive factor. And if your job is entry level - which most jobs are out of college - you're not making that much money. You may get the credit, but from the example above you're getting screwed.

What's the solution if you find yourself in such a no-win situation? Clean up your credit report. Quickly order a copy from the three credit reporting agencies below: Equifax, Experian, or Trans Union Corporation. To order your credit report from all three sources at once, in addition to your FICO score, you may order online: http://www.myfico.com. You will have access to all three reports, as well your FICO score. You will also receive an explanation of what you need to repair to raise your score. Basically, you will receive a snapshot as to how creditors view your credit worthiness.

After viewing your report carefully, search for any information that is incorrect. Sometimes credit reporting agencies make mistake. One agency reported my brother as my husband when I co-signed a car loan for him. If there are mistakes, you have the right to dispute their legitimacy, but you must do it in writing. Once the reporting agency receives your letter of dispute, they will launch an investigation. Often the credit-reporting agency will remove the offending information if they find your claim to be correct. If they are unable to verify the information, they will automatically remove the offending information from your report.

So, what does it take for one to have excellent credit? Paying bills on time and using credit wisely is a first step. Another step is the avoidance of co-signing a loan for a friend or relative. Let's say you have finally restored your credit and have a decent rating. A close friend implores you to co-sign for their new car. You ponder the thought for a moment. You know they have a steady job and can afford the monthly payment, and they really need a car. So, you relent. One sure way to lose a close friend or create tension between relatives is to co-sign for a loan and the loan goes into default because of non-payment. But I digress. Let's return to my (wink-wink)" hypothetical" situation.

The first year it's wonderful. Your friend makes their monthly payments on time. No problems. Then year two, still, no problems. But now you're segueing into year three when your friend is laid-off or becomes ill. Now they can no longer afford to make the monthly payment. They don't tell you because they're embarrassed, and the delinquent payments appear on your pristine credit report. You call your friend hoping it's a mistake, to only learn that they are having financial problems.

If the loan is a 48 or 60-month loan the bank will make you responsible for the balance of the loan. You have to pay it or suffer the consequences of repossession and a negative credit rating. Either way, their late payments are already reflected on your credit report. This act serves to lower your FICO score and return you to the high-risk category.

Another example of putting your credit at risk involves renting a car for a friend who does not have a credit card. Initially it sounds safe. You will rent the car using your card and the friends will pay cash upon the return of the car. Well, what if the friend extends the rental and doesn't tell you? What if you receive a call from the car rental agency informing you that the car is late?

You call your friend to learn they still have the car - three weeks after it was due back to the agency. After retrieving the car, you also learn that your friend is unable to pay for the rental. In most major cities, car rental rates are high. Now you're looking at a bill for $2400. You don't want to pay money for a rental you did not enjoy. Why should you pay for your friend's responsibility? In the end, who is ultimately responsible? You are always held responsible when you place your signature on a document accepting liability for payment. It does not matter if you did it for friends or relatives. If they cannot pay the bill, you will pay it, or risk ruining your credit.

So, what should one do when approached to co-sign or use their credit card for a loved one? DON'T DO IT! You'll thank me later. Just because someone has the courage to request such a request it doesn't make you obligated to appease. You must take a hard nose approach when it comes to all matters of money or business.

Just remember these six important lessons:
1. Avoid co-signing any lease or loan. Whatever the reason.
2. Never rent a car for another individual using your credit card.
3. Pay all bills on time.
4. Avoid viewing credit cards as free money and use only in emergency situations.
5. If you cannot pay the entire balance in thirty-days on your credit card do not use it for the purchase.
6. Check your credit report and FICO Score every year and clean up any inaccurate information.

To Buy or Rent? – That is the Question
When you have reached your late twenties, saving for the purchase of a home should become a priority. This will require a decision that will impact your financial future. Should you rent or own your home? The answer should be clear, but too often it is not.

After you have graduated from college and secured a job, you must begin saving money for a down payment on a piece of property. This is required for your financial stability and makes connections for generational wealth. It does not matter if you are single or married. Homeownership should be a top priority. Attempt to rent the least expensive apartment, or get a roommate, and begin to save money for a down payment for the purchase of your home.

Most home purchases will require between 5% and 10% down if the purchaser is a first-time homeowner. Otherwise, expect a 10%-20% down payment. In addition, expect a closing cost that is equivalent to 5% of the cost. There are city and government sponsored programs, along with seminars on homeownership sponsored by banks, civic and community organizations, and educational institutions available to assist with a step in this direction. Possessing a real estate and business swagger is nothing to run from. The knowledge will not only place you in the game, but also assist in ensuring financial stability.

I finally realized after paying 10 years of rent at $3000 per month, that I had basically paid for a $300,000-dollar home. Maybe not in New York City, but in many other cities where the housing market is not inflated. Homeownership would have enabled me to deduct the interest on my mortgage and reduce my tax return. Renters do not derive these deductions and subsequently throw a lot of their money out of the window. More importantly, renters do not amass equity-homeowners do.

Planning for Retirement
Although most Americans poorly plan for retirement, most African Americans are even less prepared for their post-work years, according to the Minority Retirement Confidence survey. The study, which is conducted by the American Savings Education Council attributed the reason for lack of planning by African Americans is due to the fact that they work in lower paying jobs.

African Americans are still somewhat challenged in terms of savings, particularly in lower income levels. Some are saving, but the majority are not. According to the study, 42 percent of African Americans are not confident about having enough money to live on throughout their retirement, compared to 33 percent overall. Only 59 percent of African American workers say they or their spouses have saved for retirement, compared with 71 percent of workers overall.

African Americans are also less likely to say they are offered a retirement savings plan by their current employer (58 percent vs. 73 percent). Many first-generation black investors have been frightened by the inconsistencies in the stock market. In 2007 as we entered a recession, many of us look with incredulity as white Americans talked about their loses in the stock market on national television. We felt blessed that we were not affected. But there is a lack of financial knowledge and exposure on our part that precipitated our lack of involvement.

Planning for your retirement will ensure that during your golden years you are prepared financially. Sure, social security is being deducted from your paychecks, but with the current state of the economy today who knows if social security will even be around when you're ready to retire and collect. And even if it is around have you checked your current balance and the projected amount you will receive upon retirement? Social Security alone is not enough. Therefore, it is imperative that you plan financially for your golden years.

Establishing an emergency fund is crucial for financial security. Aim to save three to six months' worth of living expenses in a readily accessible account. This fund will provide a safety net in case of unexpected events, such as job loss, medical emergencies, or major repairs. Determine what financial freedom means to you. It could involve being debt-free, having a certain level of savings or investments, or achieving a specific income level. Set short-term and long-term goals that are specific, measurable, attainable, relevant, and time-bound (SMART goals). Having clear goals will provide direction and motivation as you work towards financial freedom. Do not forget to create a will.

Creating a Will

Everyone must create a will and have it notarized. **Essence magazine** reported, "nearly 70% of African Americans have no will or estate plan in place." This leads to devastating results, including the fact "that Black Americans are missing out on the largest wealth transfer in history." As estate attorney Portia Wood said, "We are in a state of emergency now." I was amazed to learn that one of my favorite entertainers, Prince, died without a will.

Prince's estate was finalized six-years after his death. Half of his assets went to family and the other half to corporations and banks. Prince's estate was valued at $156 million dollars. Prince was not the only celebrity to die without a will, Aretha Franklin's estate was contested by her family. Having a will is essential upon death for several important reasons:

1. **Distribution of Assets**: A will allow you to specify how you want your assets and belongings to be distributed after your death. Without a will, your estate will be distributed according to the laws of intestacy, which may not align with your wishes.

2. **Control and Clarity:** With a will, you have control over who will inherit your assets, ensuring that your loved ones or beneficiaries receive what you intended for them. It provides clarity and can help prevent potential conflicts among family members.

3. **Guardianship for Minors:** If you have minor children, a will allows you to name a guardian for them. This ensures that someone you trust will take care of them in the event of your death.

4. **Minimize Legal Complications**: Having a valid will can help minimize legal complications and delays in the probate process, making it easier for your loved ones during an already difficult time.

5. **Tax Planning:** A well-structured will can include tax planning strategies to minimize estate taxes, potentially preserving more of your assets for your beneficiaries.

6. **Peace of Mind:** Creating a will provides you with peace of mind, knowing that you have made provisions for your loved ones and that your wishes will be respected after your passing.

Creating a will is crucial for asset distribution, guardianship of minors, tax planning, and reducing legal complications. Not having a will can led to contested estates and delays in the probate process. Consulting a legal professional is recommended to ensure your will aligns with your wishes and legal requirements.

Summary
- This chapter emphasizes the importance of financial freedom through assessing your situation, setting goals, and informed decisions.
- It highlights the need for continuous financial education, focusing on topics like personal finance, budgeting, investing, and money management.
- Building wealth is possible through education, entrepreneurship, and other paths, but hard work is essential.
- The challenges faced by African Americans in terms of unemployment and home foreclosures underscore the significance of financial knowledge and planning.
- The chapter also discusses the impact of financial habits on racial economic disparities, pointing out the need for wise financial choices to bridge these gaps.
- It addresses spending habits, credit scores, and investments as factors influencing financial outcomes.
- The significance of credit reports, positive credit history, and FICO scores is emphasized, as they impact loan eligibility and terms.

- The text also touches on the risks of co-signing loans and renting cars for others, highlighting the potential negative effects on credit.
- It advises against using credit cards for unnecessary purchases and encourages saving for larger expenses.
- The chapter underscores the importance of planning for retirement, establishing an emergency fund, and creating a will to ensure proper asset distribution, guardianship, and peace of mind.
- In summary, the chapter stresses the need for financial literacy, responsible financial decisions, and long-term planning to achieve financial freedom and security.

Chapter 4
Reading is Fundamental
(Literacy)

"Literacy is a bridge from misery to hope."
Kofi Annan

Reading is a wonderful gift, especially when shared with children. It nurtures imagination, essential for growth and success, and improves writing and speaking skills. It shapes intellect and emotions, forecasts possibilities, and broadens knowledge. The journey of reading can be impactful, whether across continents or just between houses. My mom made us read books regularly. We'd visit the library every two weeks, sometimes walking or biking. We'd spend hours reading, listening, and playing, leaving with 4 to 6 books each time.

At home, Mom asked about our book choices, suggesting topics like etiquette. We'd laugh, but we'd explore those subjects. Pre-Civil War, African Americans were forbidden to read, but they fought for education rights. Prominent figures like Frederick Douglass, Booker T. Washington and Mary McLeod Bethune paved the way. Reading isn't just for school; it opens new worlds and history's importance.

My mother insisted that her children read books. Every two-weeks, my younger brother, sister and I, made our way to our neighborhood library on the 2nd and 4th Saturday of every month. Sometimes we would walk. Other times we would ride our bikes. We would spend hours in the library reading books, listening to stories, and playing games. The visit would always end with our checking out 4 to 6 books.

Before the Civil War, people of African descent were not allowed to read or write. It was illegal. Early black educators felt compelled to educate its youth - but many paid a price for their efforts. Some even sacrificed their lives. As people of African descent, we have a long list of ancestors who fought and won numerous battles around inequities in education. They included Booker T. Washington, Mary McLeod Bethune, Dr. W.E.B. Dubois, Dr. Anna Julia Cooper, Thurgood Marshall, and many others.

Their successes in the courtrooms, universities, public schools, streets, and churches ensured that we had the right to literacy. Yet, there are too many not taking advantage of the right to read. Instead, they have decided to fail classes (not reading the assignments), get suspended (disrupting the class because we can't read the assignment), or simply drop out (because we refuse to learn how to comprehend what we have read).

If descendants of slaves passionately believed the only way to excel was by mastering the skill of reading - who are we to decide differently? If many taught themselves to read and sacrificed their lives to teach others - there must have been a compelling reason.

Reading is not only used for school, but as a way to travel to new places, or to present options we were unaware existed. Reading is especially necessary to understand our history. We know that schools do not teach about the importance of African Americans contributions to the foundation of this country, but we can learn by exploring various topics via reading.

Reading is a primary way to learn, gather ideas, and grasp different perspectives. It delves into science, history, and literature, expanding our understanding of the world. Reading allows us to access and absorb a vast amount of knowledge and information. It is a primary means of acquiring new ideas, facts, and perspectives on a wide range of subjects. Whether it's exploring scientific research, historical events, or literary works, reading expands our understanding of the world and helps us stay informed.

If your mama urged you to read for knowledge, she was right. Reading is a key to success and should be a priority. African Americans have a history of fighting for education, so embracing reading is a legacy. Our lives aren't rehearsals; they're real. What you plant now will manifest later.

If you have equated intelligence and success in school as being a trait reserved solely for non-African Americans, or if you believe that intelligence isn't a black thing, you must correct this fallacy. All successful people work hard to achieve their accomplishments. At some point in your life, you must embrace the notion that we have an obligation to be successful, not only in school but also in life. It is expected. It's our legacy.

Continuing education and excelling in classes are your responsibilities. Seek guidance if needed. Opportunities await, but hard work is necessary. Our ancestors' legacy of excellence should inspire us. Rediscover this legacy and gift of knowledge through reading.

There are many opportunities available for the taking. Children and parents will have to work exceptionally hard-but the rewards will be immeasurable. Our ancestors bestowed upon us a legacy of excellence. Throughout the last 50 years, a lot of knowledge has been lost through our assimilation into mainstream society. Now is the time to rediscover our neglected legacy. The greatest gift anyone can ever give is the gift of knowledge. Knowledge is nurtured and amassed through the gift of reading.

Reading is one of the keys necessary to ensure a successful life. Chances are you do not have relatives steeped in riches that will be bestowed upon you after their death. Therefore, you will need to make your own world. In order to make this world, you will need a vision. A goal. Where do you want to go? Reading will assist you in visualizing your journey.

After you have visualized your world, the next phase requires identifying the necessary stages of progress. If you become uncertain, you should seek assistance from an expert. An expert is defined as someone who has traveled the path you have carved out for yourself. Never be afraid to ask questions. Always remind yourself that knowledge is power. Enjoy the journey. Pick up all necessary tools to make it less arduous. And read as many books on the subject that is possible. If you do not have the money to buy the books-libraries still exist. Go in, apply for a card, and let the journey begin.

Once in the library or bookstore, you will meet others who share your goal of expanding their knowledge. Back in the 1970's, we would go to the library to read, and socialize with our friends. It was the spot. Young people engaged in intellectual dialogue. Friends would share plots from books they had read, and this would encourage us to read the book next. And we did not call ourselves nerds, bookworms or other condescending names. We were simply enthralled by the worlds created and explored in books.

The award-winning playwright, August Wilson, often shared stories about his passion for reading. Wilson dropped out of high school at the age of fifteen. Instead of attending school, he spent his days in the Carnegie Public Library in Pittsburgh. He began his journey by reading a Collection of Poetry by Paul Laurence Dunbar. Often, when queried about his education he would respond that he received his high school education from reading books at the library and was disappointed that more people had not taken advantage of their local libraries.

Today, the late **August Wilson** is renowned for his writing genius and his commitment to celebrate and document the black experience on stage via his ten cycle plays: *Jitney, Ma Rainey's Black Bottom, Fences, Seven Guitars, King Hedley, Gem of the Ocean, The Piano Lesson, Two Trains Running, Joe Turner's Come and Gone, and Radio Golf.* On October 16, 2005, the Broadway community dimmed the lights on the eve of his passing. Today, August Wilson was the first artist of African-decent to has a Broadway theatre named in his honor – the August Wilson Theatre.

Dr. Ben Carson's mother's mandate of reading led him to excel and become a renowned neurosurgeon. As a young boy growing up in Detroit, young Ben was having problems in school. His mother knew her son was smarter than his grades reflected on his report card. She turned off the television and mandated that he read two books a week. He later became number one in his class. Carson graduated from Yale University and the University of Michigan medical school. Presently, he is director of pediatric neurosurgery at John Hopkins Hospital in Baltimore.

Dr. Carson made history when he separated two twins who were conjoined at the head. Ben Carson was considered at-risk in school based on his economic station in life, as are many children of African - descent. Yet, his mother possessed the intellect to say failure is not an option for her son. The Carson family was economically poor - yet his mother knew there was something better in store for her son and encouraged him to discover it by supplementing his public-school education with reading books.

There are so many individuals whose life you and your progeny should know something about. These individuals have lived challenging, triumphant, and tumultuous lives, and they achieved tremendous successes through pursuing higher education. Their lives inform us of our possibilities. Their lives allow us to view the world through very unique experiences. And once we begin to see different aspects of the world, we become more aware of the infinite possibilities.

I have listed books that I believe you should have read or should read. If you missed reading any of them - better late than never- read them now. The stories serve to amplify moments in our history. The tapestries of the stories are rich with our culture, successes, and failures. The first set of books are considered classics. The second set of books are more contemporary. Read as many as you can.

Recommended Books

Manchild in the Promised Land	Claude Brown
The Autobiography of Malcolm X	Malcolm X
The Narrative of Frederick Douglass	Frederick Douglass
Their Eyes Were Watching God	Zora Neale Hurston
A Raisin in the Sun	Lorraine Hansberry
Ten Plays by August Wilson	August Wilson
The Bluest Eye	Toni Morrison
The Invisible Man	Ralph Ellison
The Poetry of Langston Hughes	Langston Hughes
The Miseducation of the Negro	Carter G. Woodson
Life Lit by Some Higher Vision	Ossie Davis

Before the Mayflower	Lerone Bennett Jr.,
I Know Why the Caged Bird Sings	Maya Angelou
Native Son/Black Boy	Richard Wright
Go Tell It on The Mountain	James Baldwin
The Collected Poems by Langston Hughes	Langston Hughes
Sula	Toni Morrison
The Color Purple	Alice Walker
The Women of Brewster Place	Gloria Naylor
Devil in a Blue Dress	Walter Mosley
The Selected Poems of Nikki Giovanni	Nikki Giovanni

Contemporary Authors

These nine prolific contemporary African American authors have made indelible contributions to literature, captivating readers with their exceptional storytelling, insightful observations, and bold exploration of complex themes. Through their works, they challenge societal norms, illuminate marginalized experiences, and inspire empathy and understanding. As we celebrate their achievements, it is crucial to continue embracing and amplifying diverse voices in literature, ensuring a vibrant and inclusive literary landscape for generations to come. If you are able, purchase the titles below you should as they will become a vital part of your home library.

Ta-Nehisi Coates	Between the World and Me
Jesmyn Ward	Sing, Unburied, Sing
Jacqueline Woodson	Brown Girl Dreaming
Chimamanda Ngozi Adichie	Americanah
Yaa Gyasi	Homegoing
Jason Reynolds	Ghost
Brit Bennett	The Mothers
N. K. Jemisin	Broken Earth
Kiese Laymon	Heavy: An American Memoir

In 2000, MTV presented a TV show that featured tours of the private homes of celebrities. My students watched it fervently and I always want to know how the media is influencing our young minds. The premise of the program involved celebrities showing off the material things they possessed in their homes. They bragged about their cars, pools, and special features like a bowling alley, or a tennis/basketball court. What always amazed me was the fact that none of them were proud of or showed-off their private library. They did not have a library.

I watched more episodes and discovered that having a library was not an integral part of their home. Some of the celebrities even had a dance pole for their female friends, but no libraries. I was stunned. A great many of our young people receive their life lessons from TV, music and social media. If celebrities are not singing or rapping about it – it becomes null and void. If images portrayed on social media and TV of black teens are conveyed as being hood or keepin' it real - which side do you think they are going to choose?

Reading is instrumental in developing language and communication skills. It exposes us to diverse vocabulary, sentence structures, and writing styles, enhancing our ability to express ourselves effectively. Reading also improves comprehension, critical thinking, and analytical skills, enabling us to understand and interpret complex ideas and arguments.

Engaging in reading exercises our cognitive abilities. It stimulates mental processes such as memory, attention, and concentration. Reading challenges our thinking, encourages problem-solving, and enhances our ability to reason and make connections. It promotes intellectual growth, expands our cognitive capacities, and can improve overall cognitive function.

Reading fuels our imagination and creativity. Books transport us to different places, time periods, and perspectives. It evokes vivid mental imagery, allowing us to visualize characters, settings, and events. This imaginative immersion cultivates creativity and inspires us to think beyond the confines of our own experiences.

If you have stopped reading or have not read a book in a long time - now is the time to return to it. The best role model for any child is their parent or adult family members. If you read, your children will read. If you spend your spare time doing things that do not encourage excellence why would you expect it of your child? Reading stimulates brain activity, and it is something that you do not need to be wealthy to enjoy. You only need your company, some light, a comfortable seat and a book. We should never forget that reading is a gift bestowed upon us from our ancestors.

Summary
- The chapter emphasizes the importance of reading, especially when shared with children, for nurturing imagination, improving skills, and broadening knowledge.
- My mother encouraged regular library visits, sparking a love for reading.
- The text underscores the historical struggles of African Americans to attain education rights, highlighting figures like Frederick Douglass and Mary McLeod Bethune.
- Reading is presented as a tool to explore new worlds, understand history, and gain knowledge.
- Success stories like August Wilson and Dr. Ben Carson demonstrate the impact of reading on achieving excellence.
- The chapter suggests recommended books and contemporary authors, showcasing the role of reading in intellectual development.
- The text concludes by stressing that reading is a gift from ancestors and encourages parents to set an example by reading.

Chapter 5
Living Longer
(Health)

"He who has health has hope, and he who has hope has everything."
Arabian Proverb

During the era of African enslavement on plantations, food scarcity led to the consumption of unappealing animal parts like intestines, feet, tongues, and tails. Despite historical inventiveness, continuing to celebrate unhealthy dishes today is unwise. Longevity necessitates a healthy diet and regular exercise, both of which should not be taken for granted.

Shifting away from family dinners to fast-food diets has become commonplace, especially among teens in areas like Harlem. Such diets often consist of items like McDonald's, Chinese food, sandwiches on white bread, soda, chips, and pizza. Nutritious options like fresh fruits and vegetables are usually absent, with urban stores offering limited healthy choices. The ongoing process of gentrification in urban neighborhoods, however, has begun to introduce healthier food options.

Exercise is crucial not just for appearance, but for maintaining overall health. Engaging in activities like running, basketball, racket ball, tennis, and swimming is important not only for physical well-being but also for a stronger heart. Since heart issues often stem from unhealthy dietary habits, exercise becomes essential in maintaining cardiovascular health.

Exercise is a vital component of a healthy lifestyle, with numerous benefits for our physical, mental, and cognitive well-being. Regular physical activity promotes physical health, boosts mental well-being, enhances cognitive function, and contributes to longevity and an improved quality of life. By incorporating exercise into our daily routines, we can experience these positive effects and lead happier, healthier lives. It is never too late to start exercising and reap the rewards it offers.

Understanding food labels is a valuable skill that shouldn't be exclusive to a certain group. Reading labels helps assess calorie, fat, sodium, and carbohydrate content, promoting good nutritional health. Neglecting proper diet and exercise can lead to health problems, such as heart disease and diabetes. African Americans are particularly susceptible to heart disease, which can result in fatal outcomes. **Diabetics may require daily injections of insulin or left untreated can** lead to loss of extremities (feet, toes and etc.). There are solutions to avoid the health issues associated with poor outcomes. Having diabetics and high blood pressure, being obese, are factors that can lead to a stroke or an early death.

The American Heart Association highlights stroke risk factors, including heredity, natural processes, and lifestyle choices. High blood pressure, cigarette smoking, high blood cholesterol, poor diet, physical inactivity, and obesity are modifiable factors that can influence stroke risk. High blood pressure, in particular, is a significant risk factor, and its damaging effects on the heart and body make it crucial to manage.

High Blood Pressure
Blacks are more likely than any other groups to have high blood pressure. High Blood Pressure (hypertension) can kill you. Left untreated, high blood pressure can cause heart disease, stroke, heart attacks and heart failure, kidney disease, sexual dysfunction and early death. High blood pressure can be prevented and controlled. Blood pressure is a measure of how hard the blood pushes against the walls of your arteries as it moves through your body. It is normal for blood pressure to go up and down throughout the day, but if it stays up, you have high blood pressure.

When blood pressure is high, it starts to damage the blood vessels, the heart, eyes and kidneys. This can lead to heart attack, stroke, and other problems. High blood pressure is called the silent killer because it doesn't usually cause symptoms while it is causing the damage.

The causes of high blood pressure include being overweight, drinking too much alcohol, having a family history of high blood pressure, eating too much salt, eating processed foods, lack of exercise, and getting older. You can prevent high blood pressure by losing weight, eating less salt, exercising at least 30-minutes a day, limiting alcohol to 2 drinks a day, eating foods rich in calcium and potassium, and following a diet rich in vegetables, grains, and fruits.

Monitor your Numbers

Blood Pressure is the force of your blood pushing against the walls of your arteries. Blood Pressure is measured with two numbers. It is written with one number over the other, such as 115/75. (See chart below.)

Blood Pressure Levels	Optimal The Goal for Most People	Pre-Hypertension On the way to High Blood Pressure	Hypertension High Blood Pressure
Systolic Top Number Heart pumps blood	Below 120	120 to 139	140 or higher
	And	Or	Or
Diastolic Bottom Number Heart relaxes	Below 80	80 to 89	90 or higher

Both systolic (top) and diastolic (bottom) numbers are important. When either number is too high, the category changes. For examples: if your blood pressure is 119/92, you have high blood pressure because the bottom number is too high (even though the top number is okay). High blood pressure is the most controllable risk factor for stroke.

Diabetes

Diabetes, a chronic health condition affecting energy conversion, is more prevalent among African Americans. Diabetes-related death rates are higher for African Americans compared to other groups. Risk factors for diabetes include obesity, hypertension, high cholesterol, and smoking. Treating diabetes with medication is common but using food as medicine is a healthier approach. Risk factors related to diabetes include obesity, hypertension, high cholesterol and cigarette smoking. Some people treat their diabetics with medication. One should always use their food as medicine instead of using their medicine as food.

Smoking
Cigarette smoking, a known risk factor for stroke, damages the cardiovascular system. The nicotine in cigarettes is addictive and contributes to cravings. Eliminating nicotine from cigarettes would impact the tobacco industry's profits, making quitting smoking challenging. Despite this, breaking the habit adds years to life.

The tobacco industry has known for years that cigarettes were addictive and therefore dangerous. Nicotine is the addictive agent in cigarettes that motivates an individual to crave more cigarettes. If nicotine was removed from cigarettes most smokers would become nonsmokers and the tobacco industry would lose billions of dollars. A small number of smokers who smoke nicotine free or natural cigarettes would remain loyal.

Because nicotine is an addictive drug, communities would become flooded by nicotine addicts. If you do not smoke, you should remain smoke free. If you do smoke, you should look for assistance in breaking the habit. You will add years to your life. And as we all know - life is already too short.

Cholesterol
Cholesterol is a naturally occurring fatty substance that plays vital roles in the body. The fat and cholesterol you eat are absorbed in the intestine and transported to the liver. High levels of LDL cholesterol are linked to atherosclerosis, which is the accumulation of cholesterol-rich fatty deposits in arteries. This can cause arteries to narrow or become blocked, slowing or stopping the flow of blood to vital organs, especially the heart and brain.
Atherosclerosis is a disease that affects the heart. It is a coronary artery disease, and it can cause a heart attack. When atherosclerosis blocks arteries that supply blood to the brain, it can also cause a stroke. You may help to prevent high cholesterol by staying on a healthy diet. This means switching from high fat foods

(eggs, fatty red meats, palm or coconut oil, dairy products made with whole milk) to fresh fruits and vegetables, whole grain breads and cereals, and low-fat dairy products.

Healthy Diets

Diets high in saturated fats, trans fat and cholesterol can raise blood cholesterol levels. Diets high in sodium (salt) can contribute to increase blood pressure. Diets with excess calories can contribute to obesity.

The National Cholesterol Education program recommends the following diet:
- Saturated fat – less than 7% of calories
- Monounsaturated fat – about 20% of calories
- Polyunsaturated fat – about 10% of calories
- Protein – about 15% of calories
- Carbohydrates – about 50% of calories
- Fiber – about 25 grams per day
- Cholesterol – less than 200 milligrams per day

Obesity

To maintain a desirable weight, you should take in only as many calories as you burn each day. If you need to lose weight, you need to take in fewer calories than you burn. Being inactive, obese, or both can increase your risk of high blood pressure, high blood cholesterol, diabetes, heart disease and stroke.

Many people of African descent have become inactive and have allowed their bodies to add unnecessary pounds. This extra weight creates many hardships for our health. Now we have to ingest chemicals or undergo surgeries to correct diseases or heal disorders that should not have been allowed to exist in the first place. We are constantly making excuses for our state of health. When you are ignorant about something – you are excused once, but after that bout with ignorance you are required to research and find the answer. Maintaining a healthy lifestyle is a requisite for maintaining longevity to enjoy the world we have created for ourselves.

Summary

- The chapter discusses the historical context of African enslavement and its impact on dietary practices, emphasizing the need for healthier food choices and exercise for longevity.
- It highlights the shift towards fast-food diets among teens in urban areas and explores the importance of exercise in maintaining overall health, especially heart health.
- The chapter also emphasizes the significance of understanding food labels and the risks associated with poor diets and lack of exercise.
- It delves into stroke risk factors, focusing on high blood pressure, and provides insights into the risks of diabetes, smoking, and high cholesterol.
- The chapter concludes by stressing the importance of healthy diets, monitoring cholesterol, and combating obesity to ensure a longer and healthier life.

Chapter 6
Black Families
(*Responsibility*)

"Our black families have persevered through centuries of challenges, displaying the power of love, solidarity and determination."
Unknown

Selecting our birth family isn't within our control, and the harmony among siblings isn't guaranteed. Hence, understanding, supporting, and loving one another becomes crucial, along with passing down these values to our own children. This requires active direction through words and actions. Ultimately, it's about those who love and are loved by us. Establishing a strong and nurturing family isn't easy, but it's essential.

At the inception of slavery, black fathers were quickly separated from their families. Whether it was during the journey through the Middle Passages, or once the ships were docked and they were sold into slavery – families were robbed of the patriarch. This injustice signaled the onset of the black, single – parent households. Mothers, absent their companions, were forced to forge a plan to keep the remaining family intact. The tradition of black women as matriarch of the family slowly took its inevitable roots.

The systems that were put in place during slavery and at the onset of reconstruction have remained strategically in place into current times. This form of systemic racism can also be attributed to the imprisonment of black men for marginal crimes. Or even worst, when history details the number of black people, over 4000, who were lynched from 1911 to 1963 - it is astounding. We will never know the exact number of lynching that took place as many were never reported or were not classified as lynching.

Economic disparities, limited opportunities, and unequal access to education exacerbate the likelihood of criminal involvement. Furthermore, the enforcement of drug laws disproportionately impacts black communities, leading to higher arrest rates. Racial profiling, discriminatory policing practices, and disparities in sentencing have been well-documented. Studies have shown that black individuals are more likely to be stopped, arrested, and receive harsher sentences compared to their white counterparts for similar offenses.

The enforcement of drug laws has disproportionately affected black communities. Despite similar rates of drug use across racial groups, black individuals are more likely to be arrested and incarcerated for drug-related offenses. This disparity has contributed significantly to the overrepresentation of black males in the criminal justice system.

Unfortunately, some fathers are unable to financially support their families due to limited job opportunities. Troubled relationships between parents can also contribute to family breakdowns. Establishing a balanced, harmonious household requires discussing traditions, expectations, education, finances, commitment, and loyalty.

Facts
- 31% of all children regardless of race live in homes without fathers.
- 80% of all African American children will spend part of their childhood living apart from their fathers.
- 38.7% of Black children live with both parents.
- 70% of black children are born to unmarried mothers

What does the above data tell us? Children raised outside of a two-parent household are:
- Five times more likely to be poor
- Twice as likely to drop out of school
- Two to three times more likely to commit crimes that lead to incarceration
- Will face an increased risk of psychological, academic, and health problems.

The outcomes of a single-parent household should be considered as we make choices for our lives and that of our progeny. Knowing some of the statistical facts should assist when making decisions about our futures.

Cultural pride is essential. Overcoming the psychological impact of slavery is crucial for black Americans to evolve and overcome adversity. Although history has devastated the black family, understanding this experience shouldn't hinder growth. It's time to break the chains and reconstruct and strengthen the black family.

Growing up without a parent can affect one's ability to navigate life. Exposure to media and entertainment shapes perceptions, and absent fathers impact girls' relationships with men. Boys need fathers to understand their roles as fathers, uncles, brothers, and husbands. Balanced households, with both parents, foster healthy development.

While some succeed despite absent fathers, their presence is vital. To improve future generations, develop cultural pride, honor parents, listen to elders, and grow individually. Parenting is challenging, especially for teen parents. Stable families, including extended ones, and responsible fatherhood play pivotal roles.

Children need a balanced household – which includes a mother and father. Young girls need their father to help develop a healthy relationship to men. Adult women openly express missed opportunities in not having their father at home. Some described the fact that they have never met their dad. The sorrow and pain are always evident when they describe their fantasies of having a father in their life, or how they wish they knew their father.

Consequently, women who do not have a father often make unhealthy choices in their selection of a companion. Subconsciously, the missed opportunity of having a father can translates into them staying in an abusive and unfulfilling relationship. On the surface, they believe any man is better than no man at all. They missed the lesson in terms of what they should expect from a man because they have not witnessed a healthy relationship in motion.

Fathers are just as important to the structure of the family as the mother. Bitterness and disappointment are the emotions often expressed when conveying the loss or absence of a relationship. Boys need their fathers to define their role as fathers, uncles, brothers, and husbands. It is never too late for a father to reclaim his child. There are situations where a father, estranged from his companion, desires a relationship with his child but is forbidden by the mother. Women should do what will be in the best interest of their child. If the relationship or marriage ends, women should allow their children to have a healthy relationship with their dad.

Living in a balanced and healthy household are the necessary components of enjoying a fulfilling and successful life. Granted, there are examples of excellence from individuals who have achieved success with an absentee father. But this should not be the norm. A father's presence ensures so many healthy facets to an individual's life. A father's role should never be taken for granted.

If you are disappointed with your family life - work to ensure that the next generation is different. Work on improving who you are as an individual so that you are able to reach your goals. Insist that your children always honor and respect their parents, as well as other adults. Teach them to listen to their elder's life stories, learn from them, and grow.

The responsibilities faced by parents are arduous. Parenting children when you are financial stable is already a challenge. Attempting to raise a child before you have completed high school or college is understandably the most difficult challenge one can face in their life. But if the children are already here - lamenting your situation is too late. You have to take the ball and get your family's life rolling in a positive direction.

Teen parents have not lived and experienced the world profoundly enough to share their wisdom with their offspring. They are still growing and developing a clear understanding of the world. This limited life experiences make their perspective somewhat limited. Their child will automatically be set-up for failure, unless they too learn how to raise a successful child. Otherwise, this failure will spring forth a host of obstacles they might continue from one generation to the next and it may never be overcome.

Summary
- This chapter discusses the importance of understanding, supporting, and loving family members.
- It highlights the challenges faced by black families due to historical events like slavery and systemic racism, leading to single-parent households.
- Systemic racism within the criminal justice system contributes to the overrepresentation of black males in prisons.
- Economic disparities, limited opportunities, and unequal access to education also contribute to criminal involvement.
- Single-parent households impact children's futures, leading to increased likelihood of poverty, dropouts, and psychological challenges.
- Cultural pride is crucial for overcoming adversity. Growing up without a parent affects one's life navigation and relationships.
- The presence of fathers is vital for healthy development.
- Planning parenthood and responsible fatherhood are emphasized to break the cycle and raise successful children.

Chapter 7
What About Love?
(Relationships)

*"What's love, but a secondhand emotion?
What's love got to do with it?
Who needs a heart when a heart can be broken?"*
Tina Turner

The complex emotion of love has captivated hearts across history, inspiring art, literature, and music. Its transformative impact on individuals and societies is undeniable. Love is multifaceted, holding the power to change lives. Healthy relationships are invaluable, and we mustn't take them for granted.

Many people have lived without the solace of love. Did they not yearn for companionship? Were they undeserving? Why were they denied? The reasons may remain elusive, but those fortunate to find love without complications are truly lucky.

During my University of Michigan freshman years, I observed that most girls sought boyfriends on campus. Amidst the pursuit of education, some sought life partners, while others aimed to balance both. The right path varies due to personal choices.

Mothers often share their experiences with daughters. Limited experiences lead to limited advice, and complete, loving families foster positive examples. Observing healthy relationships is vital, yet often overlooked. Tips get ignored during this crucial phase. A classmate's mother advised her to find a husband in college, warning of limited options post-graduation. Love, she believed, was based on myths. Today, my friend is contentedly married with a family. Others, however, were skeptical about love.

The innate human need for companionship is undeniable. Connecting with others is natural, whether as spouses, significant others, or soulmates. We all desire to love and be loved.

Love is portrayed in music, movies, TV, ads, and literature. Media encourages romantic fantasies, often accompanied by easy-to-follow directions for happiness. From childhood, kids sense attraction without fully understanding it. Adults label these feelings as crushes, nurturing the idea of romantic relationships.

Romantic love, depicted in literature and films, involves deep emotional and sexual attraction. It ranges from infatuation's exhilaration to the stability of long-term commitment. Love brings joy, vulnerability, and potential heartbreak.

Young girls indulge in Cinderella fantasies, believing love completes them. They strive for attractiveness, spending more time on grooming. Boys, on the other hand, select girls for peer perception. Boys' motives often revolve around societal expectations of fatherhood.

Many women, especially those over 40, still await their Prince Charming. Some prepared by excelling academically, staying fit, and achieving success. They altered appearances to match perceived desires. Yet, some men lacked ambition, blaming society. The concept of love is diverse and varies between genders. Regardless, the pursuit of love remains an integral part of human existence.

MICHELLE and LEONARD – Case Study

Michelle was an eighteen-year-old sophomore in college when she realized that most of the girls on her college campus were strategically aligning their focus on snagging a boyfriend who could later become their husband. This was in addition to graduating from college. Michelle was somewhat out of the loop because her goals did not include seeking a husband. Her focus was on having a strong undergraduate transcript to ensure that she would later get accepted into law school.

Michelle studied doing the week, as well as most weekends. She also actively participated in weekly study groups with her peers. Males flirted with her most of the time, but she often ignored their advances. Michelle viewed men as a distraction. Her mother's voice often rang loudly in her ears "all they want to do is get you pregnant and leave you." And Michelle certainly did not want any children - especially at eighteen. But the pressure to date was beginning to creep into Michelle's world. She fought it as long as she could until the day, she met Leonard.

Leonard was two years older than Michelle and had recently dropped out of college. This fact he kept from Michelle until much later in their relationship. Leonard had a decent paying job with the promise of advancement and opportunities. On top of all of this, Leonard was a player, and he knew it. A long-term relationship was not on his radar. He simply loved the ladies.

Michelle eventually realized Leonard's lack of goals by the fact that he had dropped out of college. She then encouraged him to return to college, all to no avail. The only thing that was certain was Michelle was attracted to Leonard. Everything in Michelle's psyche' told her to leave him alone, but her animalistic instincts told her differently and she gave in to his advances.

It wasn't long before Leonard was encouraging Michelle to skip classes by inviting her to see a movie or have lunch during class time. New to relationships, Michelle did not see a developing pattern. She simply concluded that she had fallen in love with Leonard. And everything she had read in books supported her conclusion.

Then, one year into the relationship, Michelle's grades began to drop. One afternoon, one of her professors called her into her office to discuss her performance and attendance. Michelle made excuses and promised to change and resume her high standards. When her mother saw her grades, she scolded Michelle for succumbing to a man. She chastised Michelle for not being the independent woman she thought she had reared. Michelle resented her mother's lectures and grew closer to Leonard.

Leonard's mother, on the other hand, was ecstatic that her son had hooked a smart and attractive girlfriend. She was certain that Michelle would provide the impetus for her son to get back on track and complete his education. Leonard had the intelligence to complete college but had not been motivated. Here was an opportunity for him to get it together. If the scenario had proven successful Michelle and Leonard would become a happy and successful couple.

Eventually Michelle grades dropped lower and lower and she was dismissed from college. Her mother was highly disappointed but said nothing to her daughter who was forced to return home and look for a job. Leonard remained in the college town and began to date other women. His visits to Michelle began to diminish and Michelle sunk into a depression.

Leonard was sighted by many of Michelle's friends with various women. Michelle began to understand why he had minimized visits. Then Michelle began to gain weight. When Leonard would visit, he often complained about her size and even told her that her new weight was the reason he had begun to date other women.

Ten years later, Michelle was still single and was not the lawyer she had planned to become. Whereas Leonard eventually returned to school, received his degree, married and lived happily ever after.

What went wrong?
Women believe men have it easier because they choose the woman. But if you ask any man, he will tell you that it is the woman who has it easiest because she has to agree to the courtship. Therein lies the confusion. Who is right? Does life really amount to being single or married? Is that the real meaning of life? Should our lives consist of searching for love and everything else is secondary?

We must stay focused on our personal goals regardless of the obstacles. Having a companion is wonderful but should not define or cause us to give-up on long planned goals. If we are going to deviate from the path it should be for reasons that add to our life and not subtract. Life is rather short, and the best years are truthfully spent while one is young. As we mature, we obtain degrees of wisdom based on our experiences or from the experiences of others. Most young people fail to listen to wiser and caring adults because they believe that was then and this is now. Things have changed. But have they?

Both women and men should listen to the intelligence and wisdom of their elders, parents, and extended family. Usually, they have walked the path before and can warn of dangerous and treacherous waters. You are never too old to listen to the advice of seasoned adults. This advice often leads to ensuring that an individual has completed their goals and have a sense of where they want to go.

If we believe we know it all, we are setting ourselves up for major disappointments in life. Having a companion can offer much in terms of support both spiritually and economically. Raising a family can be joyous with a partner but can also bring disappointments. We have to know who we are first before we connect with another. You are encouraged to make a plan for your life that simply relies on you.

According to Webster's dictionary love is defined as "an intense feeling of tender affection and compassion, or a passionate feeling of romantic desire and sexual attraction." Who would not want to experience love? Most people want to experience love, but sometimes it can come disguised in the form of dependency on another. If you are fortunate and attract a healthy loving relationship count your blessings. Never take it for granted. Nurture and be protective of the relationship because there are no guarantees that it will last forever.

Always love, protect, and nurture yourself. If you take care of yourself in a positive manner, you are guaranteed to attract a healthy and supportive companion into your life. On the other hand, if you spend too much time on the wrong things or celebrate a relationship that does not bring healthy aspects into your life - it is not love, but an obsession.

Obsessions are not only unhealthy but have the ability to waste your time. No one has time to waste. Never allow an obsession to rob you of precious time. Love is a wonderful addition in all of our lives, but always discern when it is legitimate love and not an obsession. Always believe that you deserve the best – because you are worth it.

Love, in all its forms, holds immense significance in our lives. It enriches our relationships, fuels personal growth, and promotes compassion and altruism.

From romantic love to the love shared within families and the broader compassion we extend to humanity; love plays a pivotal role in shaping our experiences and the world around us. By embracing love, practicing empathy, and fostering meaningful connections, we can create a more harmonious and compassionate society. Let us cherish and celebrate the transformative power of love in our lives.

Summary
- This chapter delves into the multifaceted nature of love, which has been a timeless source of inspiration in art, literature, and music.
- The profound impact of love on individuals and societies is emphasized, highlighting its transformative power.
- The value of healthy relationships is underscored, emphasizing the need to appreciate and not take them for granted.
- The narrative discusses the experiences of individuals who have lived without the presence of love and companionship.
- It raises questions about their longing for connection and the reasons behind their deprivation.
- The narrative acknowledges that finding uncomplicated love is a stroke of luck.
- An observation is shared from my time at the University of Michigan in the 1980s, noting the varying paths pursued by girls in terms of seeking romantic relationships or focusing on education. The influence of personal choices in this regard is acknowledged.
- The role of mothers in passing down relationship advice and experiences is explored. Limited experiences can lead to restricted advice, while complete and loving families serve as positive examples.
- The importance of observing healthy relationships is emphasized, and the overlooking of crucial relationship advice during pivotal phases is highlighted.
- The chapter explores how children experience attraction and how adults label these feelings, shaping the notion of romantic relationships.

- Romantic love, as depicted in literature and films, is explored, covering its emotional and sexual aspects. The range from infatuation's exhilaration to the stability of long-term commitment is discussed, acknowledging the spectrum of emotions it brings.
- The chapter also addresses the differing views of young girls and boys towards romantic relationships. It discusses how girls often idealize love, while boys may be influenced by peer perceptions and societal expectations.
- The chapter concludes by considering the experiences of women over 40 who still await a fulfilling relationship. The influence of societal expectations and personal preparation is noted, as well as the idea that some men lack ambition due to societal factors.
- In summary, this chapter delves into the complex nature of love and relationships. It explores personal experiences, observations, and societal influences that shape people's understanding and pursuit of love, ultimately highlighting the universal human desire for meaningful connections.

Chapter 8
What about God?

(Spirituality)

"In the beginning was the Word, and the Word was with God, and the Word was God."
John 1:1.

Throughout history, the question of a higher power, often called God, has sparked much debate and thought. While opinions on God can be deeply personal, it's crucial to approach the topic with an open mind, acknowledging the various viewpoints that people hold around the world.

I can fondly recall reading stories about Adam and Eve, Moses, Noah's Ark and Jesus when I was a child. I remember one Christmas asking my mother for an anthology of bible stories. I would read each story with the fervor of a child reading comic books. I was fascinated by the journeys of the characters and how God had a hand in each situation.

My siblings and I were especially drawn to religious movies. The Ten Commandments with Charlton Heston and King of Kings with Jeffrey Hunter were family favorites. Spirituality and a relationship with God were always present in our home. Every Sunday morning, Aretha Franklin's magnificent album, Amazing Grace, filled our house. My mother, a former gospel singer, loved gospel music and we, being her children, loved it as well.

Growing up in Detroit, our family attended church weekly. My grandfather had been a deacon in his small church in Arkansas and my mother grew up knowing God's words. As an extension of her upbringing, we were expected to know his words too. Did it damage us to be mandated to attend church on Sunday? Or bible school for five-weeks every summer? Not really. Were we thrilled to sing in the choir? Or perform in the Easter Pageants? Yes. Did it help steer us clear of jail time, using drugs, or being teen parents? Some would say yes.

Whether you follow Christianity, Judaism, Catholicism, Hinduism, Buddhism, Islam, or any other religion, exploring spirituality and sharing it with the next generation is crucial. It can help shape their growth. The idea of worship in places like churches, synagogues, mosques, or temples is comforting for many. Some see faith in a higher being as natural as breathing.

Belief in God is deeply personal and varies greatly from person to person. For many, the concept of God provides a source of comfort, meaning, and guidance in their lives. Spirituality offers a framework for understanding the world, one's purpose, and the moral values by which they choose to live. These beliefs often stem from religious teachings, spiritual experiences, or a combination of both. It is essential to respect and appreciate the diversity of individual beliefs and the role it plays in shaping one's identity and worldview.

While many embrace the belief in God, skepticism and atheism also exist as valid viewpoints. Skeptics question the existence of a higher power, often seeking empirical evidence to support their perspectives. Atheists, on the other hand, assert that there is no God or higher power. These perspectives often arise from philosophical reasoning, scientific inquiry, or personal experiences that lead individuals to question or reject the notion of a divine being. Understanding these perspectives is essential to engage in respectful dialogues that promote intellectual growth and mutual understanding.

Belief in God, or the absence thereof, has far-reaching implications for individuals and society. Personal faith can provide individuals with solace during challenging times, foster a sense of community through religious gatherings, and inspire acts of compassion and charity.

Religion also plays a significant role in shaping cultural values, ethical frameworks, and social norms. However, differences in religious beliefs can also lead to conflicts, discrimination, and the marginalization of certain groups. Nurturing a society that respects diverse beliefs, promotes dialogue, and upholds principles of equality and mutual understanding is crucial in fostering social harmony.

If your parents didn't guide your spirituality, you can develop your own belief system. Faith is vital for compassion. Communities are built through shared practices, and culture is reinforced through worship. Parents use teachings as a guide for raising children.

The concept of God is a deeply complex and multifaceted aspect of human existence. Personal beliefs, religious traditions, skepticism, and atheism all contribute to the diversity of perspectives surrounding this topic. It is important to approach discussions about God with respect, empathy, and an open mind, recognizing the significance of these beliefs for individuals and the impact they have on society. By fostering understanding and promoting dialogue, we can navigate this intricate topic in a way that encourages mutual respect, intellectual growth, and a deeper appreciation for the diversity of human spirituality.

Summary

- The essay explores the concept of a higher power, often referred to as God, throughout history.
- It emphasizes the importance of approaching the topic with an open mind due to the diversity of viewpoints.
- The author shares personal experiences, like reading religious stories and watching movies, and highlights the significance of spirituality in their family.
- The chapter discusses the role of belief in God in providing comfort, meaning, and guidance for individuals, while acknowledging skepticism and atheism as valid viewpoints.
- The impact of belief in God on individuals, society, and culture is explored, along with the importance of respectful dialogue and understanding.
- The chapter concludes by emphasizing the complex nature of the concept of God and the need for open-minded discussions that promote mutual respect and intellectual growth.

Chapter 9
If You Can Go to Jail
(Obstacles)

"Injustice anywhere is a threat to justice everywhere."
Dr. Martin Luther King, Jr.

As adolescents mature, parents take on an even more significant role. Some perceive the teenage years as personal and private, but by age twelve, a child has only experienced a small slice of life and isn't equipped to make all the major life decisions. Parents must stay involved to provide guidance and insights. Children can't know everything, and it's impossible for them to do so. As parents, it's crucial to offer advice on the choice's children will encounter.

If your child is unsuccessful - people will say, "well, what did you expect...the apple doesn't fall too far from the tree." Ultimately, you will receive the blame anyway. So, take the job of raising your children seriously. No parent desires to bury a child or raise money to bail them out of jail, or even worse watch their child being locked up for any period of time. We should look forward to celebrating the positive gains that are achieved by ourselves and our children.

We have the responsibility of preparing ourselves and our children for their role as an adult. During the teen years, there will be numerous hooks out to get and prevent us from becoming the success our ancestors and others fought for. Prisons, cemeteries, unemployment, depression, alcohol and drug abuse are elements awaiting any wrong turn on this journey called life.

Black Americans are imprisoned at an alarming rate compared to White Americans. Though comprising only 12 percent of the population, Black individuals constitute 44 percent of prisoners in the U.S. African Americans are arrested and imprisoned for drug offenses at higher rates than whites. In state prisons, 63 percent of drug offenders are Black, highlighting the stark overrepresentation within the penal system.

An analysis of the incarceration rates in the USA show a frightening picture of this nation as a locked down nation for a large segment of our population. Some interesting aspects are these:
- California, which has the sixth largest economy in the world, with a Black population that is only 7%, has a prison population that is 32% Black.

- Texas ranks number one in putting citizens to death. It has a Black population that equals 14%, yet a prison population that is 54%.
- Maryland has the largest percentage of Black prisoners – 77%.
- Mississippi, with the largest Black population of 36% has a prison population of 75%.

When raising Black children, know that the statistics are stacked against them avoiding jail or prison. Ultimately, you have the power to help chart the course of their life. You know the rules and have practiced the lessons, now is the time to share them with your offspring and yourself. You must ring the bells when you are heading in the wrong direction. Observe your child and ring the bells early in their lives. Do not wait until after they have solidified who they are in the teen years. Let them know when they are departing from the path. Stand your ground.

Ensure that you surround yourself with people who reflect the values and mores you want for your child. As the parent, a great amount of responsibility will fall on your shoulders. If you do not want your child to sell drugs or rob stores, do not have individuals in your home who represent that lifestyle. It is your child's precious life you are protecting. Encourage role models who are successful and have accomplished something. Prepare the road for your child's journey by removing all impediments.

Life Lessons – Case Study#1
There was an interesting story in Harlem that involved a creative director losing his job over a crime committed by his brother. The brother - let us call him James. James was employed in an educational institution that trained young boys to become successful musicians and vocalist and gain college acceptance. The director, let us call him Gregg, created the program, raised the money, solicited prestigious community leaders for his board of trustees, and met with corporate heads. He beat the pavement in an earnest effort to garnered support for his program. He created what would later become a national institution.

Gregg hired James to add his expertise to the organization. James was honored that he was included in the making of something special. He vowed to work tirelessly towards the vision of his brother. They worked hard and eventually involved others in the idea. The idea started to grow. It was years before they would see the fruits of their labors, but with their hard work and perseverance they moved closer and closer to their goal.

Fast-forward 25 years. Their organization had become a national treasure. It was not only known throughout the country, but throughout the world. Accolades, awards and honors were bestowed upon the organization and its founders. Performances were scheduled. Money continued to flow into the organization. Newspapers and magazines detailed stories of their climb to success despite numerous obstacles. The institution had finally arrived. They traveled around the world and created a major sensation.

The Nightmares Begin
James was accused and subsequently charged with a crime. The news had a negative impact on the world-renowned organization. The charges accused James of sexually molesting some of the young boys. James was arrested. This travesty, naturally, had a major impact on the organization. The media published stories about the alleged incidents. Despite the accolades previously showered the organization, parents quickly remove their children from the organization.

Gregg, in an effort to support his brother, borrowed money from the organization to pay his bail. And, surprisingly to all, he did not suspend him pending the outcome of the investigation and subsequent trial. He even kept him on the payroll of the organization and allowed him to travel with other students on an international tour. Gregg appreciated the work and commitment James has shared with the organization.

Now the nightmare begins to continue to spiral out of control.
One year later, James occupies a prison cell. His career is over. The spotlight and media attention now shifted its focus to Gregg. Questions were asked.

Innuendos were implied. Gregg's glory and accolades are now forgotten as his judgment and reputation are challenged. Finally, he is asked to resign his position. His organization, his baby, no longer belongs to him. He is out.

Eventually, the organization ceased to exist. When Gregg passes away a few years later, his historical contributions are overshadowed by his involvement with and support of his brother. The awards, the tours, and the performances are sadly forgotten. All of this occurred because of his involvement and support of a family member.

There are many lessons that can be learned by another person's mistakes. One lesson learned from this incident involved never putting yourself in a position that will jeopardize your job or even worse your reputation. When it is all finally said and done all you have is your reputation and your sense of ethics. Once you compromise your ethics you can basically throw away everything else.

If you are ever placed in a situation where the outcome can involve losing your job or even worse setting up temporary or permanent residence in a prison cell - you should run for the hills. You can always meet and cultivate new friends, but the years spent in prison will never be recouped. Learning a lesson while sitting in a prison cell is futile. You will give up a part of your life that you will never get back. It is lost. Gone forever.

Hanging out with friends – Case Study #2
This story involves one of my former high school students. Let's call him Paul. Paul excelled in school and was basically a well-liked young man. He stayed out of trouble and always did the right thing. One day, Paul received a phone call from a close friend, Reggie, inviting him to attend a party. Paul accepted the invitation because he always enjoyed hanging out with Reggie. When Reggie arrived at Paul's home, there was another boy seated in the passenger seat of the car, Michael. Paul felt an air of trepidation as he climbed into the back seat because he knew that Michael had spent some time locked-up. But he trusted his friend Reggie and acquiesced.

The car quickly careened down the road as the boys enjoyed the music on the radio. Their conversations were dominated by the prospect of meeting new girls at the party. About twenty-minutes into the escapade, Michael asked Reggie to stop at a store. He wanted to pick-up snacks to take to the party. Reggie pulled into the parking lot and Michael went into the store.

The Nightmare Begins
Paul and Reggie waited patiently in the car for Michael's return. Michael emerged from the store running with a security guard pursuing him. He jumped into the car and instructed Reggie to drive. Reggie conceded. Once in the car, Michael explained that the security guard was trippin' and trying to play him. So, he had to leave, but only after calling him a name, which had led to the quick exit from the store. The boys laughed at the incident and attributed it to an overzealous, "fake" cop.

Within minutes, a police car was in pursuit of the boys. Michael instructed Reggie to floor it. Connecting the event to a badge of honor that he would later brag about to his friends, Reggie relented as the car sped off. The pursuit continued as the police car accelerated its speed in pursuit of the boys. Paul continually yelled from the back seat to stop the car and let him out. His demands went unheeded.

The boys were eventually captured and placed under arrest. Paul loudly and repeatedly proclaimed his innocence. All to no avail. Reggie and Michael shared nothing to support Paul's accounting of the incident. Michael had robbed the store and shot the clerk. All three boys were found guilty and whisked off to serve a 3-5-year prison term.

Parents have an important job. Their presence is required and necessary in the lives of their children. And this job never ends. If you do work to establish mores and values in your child - who do you expect will pick up the slack? Schools have a role, the community has a role, and the church even serves a role. But ultimately the individuals responsible for ensuring that the work is being done are the parents.

Reportedly, 42 percent of black males in urban communities fail a grade at least once by the time they are in high school and 55 percent do not graduate. The expectation that your child will attend college is not on everyone's agenda. There are other factors and systems in place to catch your child if you do not do your job. The judicial system expects a high percentage of Black and Latino males to spend time in jail or prison.

The penal institution is set-up and waiting to catch your child, especially your sons, if they do not succeed in school. Gang influence or prostitution will accept your child, too. And ultimately, the mortuary science industry will appreciate the income that is generated when your child dies early due to unsupervised activities. So, it's best to prepare your son (and daughters) to avoid incidents that could cause them to fall short of their goals.

Know that the judicial system determines the number of jails to build in urban communities based on math test scores of children in the 4th grade. The institution relies on the belief that 2 out of every 4 Black and Latino males will spend time in jail or prison a minimum of 5 years. If you do not deter your boys from practicing a criminal lifestyle or possessing a thug's swagger, do not be surprised when they become exactly that.

If you live long enough everything comes full circle. Parents who are in touch with their children and provide rules and expectations rear healthy successful offspring. Children who do not respect or abide by their parent's rules are setting themselves up for trouble. You cannot imagine the number of times I hear parents say, "I can't do anything with him." They have given up and are tired of the headaches. It is understandable, but they cannot give up. No parent wants to travel across the state to visit their precious child locked up in a jail cell. Yet this happens more frequently than anyone would care to share.

The United States leads in citizen incarceration, with over two million individuals imprisoned. Most incarcerated individuals are nonwhite. It's critical to guide your children away from criminal lifestyles or thug personas to prevent their downfall.

Granted, there are examples of men who were falsely accused and imprisoned. There are also men who were jailed for standing up for their rights. There are men who reformed their lives while in prison. But that is not the case for most. History tells us that Dr. Martin Luther King Jr., was jailed advocating for our civil rights, as were many of his followers. He was always released. His incarcerations were racist and unfounded. Fast-forward 35 years.

Stanley Tookie Williams was an early leader of the Crips, a notorious street gang that had its roots in South Central, Los Angeles in 1971. In 1993, he began making changes in his behavior, and became an anti-gang activist while on Death Row. He co-wrote award-winning children's books. In his books he discouraged young males from joining gangs and following a criminal's blueprint. Mass numbers of politicians, lawyers, and entertainers advocated for his release from prison. All to no avail. In December 2005 he was executed for the murder of Albert Owens

Choosing friends and associates is a precarious responsibility. Everyone has heard the adage "birds of a feather flock together." Your mama should have told you that you are judged by the company you keep. You must teach this lesson to your children. If they are hanging out with individuals who have nothing going on in their lives – what do they hope to gain? The United States leads in citizen incarceration, with over two million individuals imprisoned. Most incarcerated individuals are nonwhite. It's critical to guide yourself and your children away from criminal lifestyles or thug personas to prevent their downfall.

Summary
- This chapter discusses the crucial role parents play in guiding their adolescent children, especially during the teenage years.

- The chapter emphasizes that, despite perceptions of privacy, parents must remain involved in their children's lives to offer guidance and insights.
- It underscores the importance of parents providing advice and direction, given that young individuals lack the experience to make major life decisions.
- The potential consequences of not guiding children through life choices are highlighted, including negative outcomes like imprisonment and ruined reputations.
- The chapter also provides case studies illustrating the impact of poor choices and associations on individuals' lives.
- It stresses the need for parents to instill values, make their expectations clear, and ensure their children associate with positive influences.
- The chapter also touches on the disproportionate incarceration rates among Black Americans and the need to guide children away from criminal behavior and negative influences.

Chapter 10
Release the Fear
(Stress)

"Lose not courage, go forward...and you will compel the world to respect you."
Marcus Garvey

Too often, we are simply afraid to desire success. We present the front that we are embarrassed to have a thirst for knowledge and excellence. Some of the fear is associated with memories of ancestors being assassinated, lynched, or having our homes burned or firebombed, schools burned to the ground, or our ancestors run out of town if they challenged the segregated laws that were installed to oppress people of African descent. To witness or learn about our exceptional leaders' assassination, or heroic civil rights workers murdered, towns burned, and churches bombed, strategically placed a quiet fear in our lives.

This phenomenon can also be traced back to our days as slaves. If a righteous slave had the intelligence to plan a revolt or hatched a plot to escape, too often fearful and passive slaves thwarted their plans. They would announce the plan to the plantation owner. In the historical examples of Nat Turner, Gabriel Prosser, and Denmark Vesey who organized slave rebellions on plantations, they were betrayed by members of their own race.

Medgar Evans assassination came after his work with the NAACP. He was instrumental in registering groups of blacks to vote. Dr. Martin Luther King Jr., and Malcolm X assassinations came after they lead massive groups of black people towards freedom and equality. Marcus Garvey was deported to Jamaica as a consequence of his persuasive expertise in motivating Africans in America to return to the Motherland. He bought a ship, The Black Star, in hopes of sailing "Back to Africa."

Many of our greatest leaders lost their lives in hopes of emancipating us and making the world a better place. They knew the various risks - yet they persevered. Inevitably, in modern times, we became afraid to challenge anything publicly, and the leaders who attempted to emerge were maligned on multiple levels. This castration relegated them powerless. The fear of being maligned and murdered for challenging the status quo has been systemically passed from generation to generation. It is deeply etched in our subconscious. Psychologically, we have been raped of our courage and pride, and what remains is fear.

Possessing knowledge of this historical reality should compel people of color to excel in spite of the current odds. We have given up, to an extent, of expecting and receiving the best. Instead, we tolerate mediocre schools. We accept crime-infested neighborhoods. We allow our boys to identify with prison and gang subcultures. We say we are keeping it real by remaining in low-income housing. We have lowered the bar for ourselves and our progeny, and now must redirect. We have forgotten from whence we came. We allow others to write our history and define our images. This system serves to direct us towards a culture that is based on street sensibilities. And these sensibilities further serve to enslave us - both spiritually and financially.

Imagining that a force of racism is set-up to hold you back is self-defeating. It is there but should not define us. Too many of us are holding ourselves back by being chained to our own apathy. Many of us are fearful of stepping up as that might lead to our demise. There are psychological fears that are embedded in our minds due to the mistreatment of those who were willing to fight for our rights. We have to release the fear and move forward.

In an era marked by social and political upheaval, a new generation of activists has emerged, using their voices, creativity, and determination to drive change in their communities and beyond. But we mustn't forget the success stories of people who overcame tremendous obstacles. Contemporary activists like Amanda Gorman, Patrisse Cullors, Bryan Stevenson, Nipsey Hussle, and Stacey Abrams show us the power of determination and courage in creating change. It's crucial to educate ourselves about the achievements of our predecessors and celebrate our accomplishments. There are others but these individuals are noteworthy.

Amanda Gorman
Amanda Gorman is a young poet and activist, captured the world's attention with her powerful words at the presidential inauguration in 2021. Gorman's advocacy focuses on issues of racial equality, women's rights, and social justice.

Her eloquent poetry has the ability to inspire and unite people from diverse backgrounds, making her a beacon of hope for positive change.

Patrisse Cullors
Co-founder of the Black Lives Matter movement, Patrisse Cullors has been at the forefront of the fight against systemic racism and police violence. Through her activism, Cullors has raised awareness about the injustices faced by Black individuals and communities. Her dedication to social justice has sparked conversations, protests, and policy changes on a global scale.

Bryan Stevenson
Bryan Stevenson, a lawyer and social justice activist, has dedicated his life to addressing issues related to racial inequality and the criminal justice system. He founded the Equal Justice Initiative, an organization that fights for fair treatment of marginalized individuals within the legal system. Stevenson's work sheds light on the disparities in sentencing, incarceration, and access to legal representation.

Nipsey Hussle
Nipsey Hussle, a rapper and community activist, used his platform to advocate for positive change in his hometown of Los Angeles. He invested in local businesses, created job opportunities, and supported educational initiatives to uplift his community. Tragically killed in 2019, Nipsey's legacy lives on through his commitment to empowering underserved neighborhoods.

Stacey Abrams
Stacey Abrams gained prominence for her advocacy in voter rights and her groundbreaking campaign for the Georgia gubernatorial race in 2018. Despite the loss, her efforts brought attention to voter suppression and inspired conversations about the importance of fair elections. Abrams continues to work tirelessly to ensure equal access to voting for all citizens.

In a world facing numerous challenges that lead to fear, the activism of the noted individuals Amanda Gorman, Patrisse Cullors, Bryan Stevenson, Nipsey Hussle, and Stacey Abrams should serve as a reminder of the power of determination, compassion, and creativity in driving positive change. Their contributions across various domains highlight the diverse ways in which contemporary activists can impact society, inspiring others to join the journey toward a more just and equitable world.

The assassinations of some of our most prominent leaders, the lynching of our fearless ancestors, and the burning of our communities has instilled a psychological fear that remains within us. Our objective has to include pushing forward and continuing a pursuit of justice for all.

Your mama should have told you about your potential for greatness. She should have told you that you have an obligation to face all of your fears and devise a plan to defeat them. She should have informed you that:

- You have the right to achieve your dreams.
- You must select friends and role models who encourage excellence in your life.
- When you achieve success, you have to turn around and determine how many you can help.
- You have to become the leader of your own life. There are examples of excellence for you to follow.

If you can uncover the source of your fear - you can move to conquer it - but understand that a great deal of it comes from your own history. If your parents did not graduate high school, they should encourage you to graduate high school. And if your parents did not attend or graduate from college – they should encourage their children, or better, encourage themselves.

When my former students would share that they did not receive any assistance from family members when exploring college options, I was somewhat baffled. In this day and time, I concluded that all parents were pushing their children towards success. As principal of a high school, I encouraged my staff to take the lead. I set-up a college mentoring program that paired 8-10 students with teachers at the beginning of their senior year. These teachers would serve as mentors to guide our students through the college process. The group would also serve as a network for the students to ask questions and share experiences.

In the absence of tradition, we are required to find or create opportunities for our own success. If your parents are apathetic towards your goals - do not process their issues. Always remember that your parent's reality is their reality. Your reality involves your attending and graduating from college and beginning a career in the profession of your choice.

If your parents are still living in low-income housing by the time you graduate high school, chances are you will repeat the pattern if you do not devise a different course for your life. No disrespect is intended to parents who take advantage of affordable housing, but how long do you plan on living there? And what messages are you sending your child? One should not expect to get through life on a hook-up. Work to achieve the things you want in life. It is not okay to accept less than what you want. Always expect the best because you deserve it.

In 1915, shortly after reconstruction, blacks began a migration from the rural south to the urban north. Their hopes included better housing, education, and job opportunities. They had received letters from relatives in the north inviting them to move up north and enjoy the pie in the sky. But when they arrived conditions were not exactly as described. Times were just as bad in the north. There were simply more people attempting to survive. Some found ways to generate income for themselves and their families. Others relied on the kindness of the government to support them financially. This Public Assistance should have been short termed.

The Welfare Initiative was created through government social programs. They were designed to assist the countless Americans, both black and white, that were unable to sustain a living. Somehow, too many of us applied for the aide without a plan to get off of the programs. You mama should have told you not to take a handout from any governmental agency. She should have told you that receiving aide without a plan and timeline is not public assistance but becomes a way of life for too many.

No longer are there incredible forces being designed to prevent you from achieving success. Yes, racism still exists in this country. But there are countless means to combat it. Apathetic people will tell you that "the man" will not allow a black man to - you fill in the dots. You have to understand that you are entitled to the riches that this country is able to afford and provide. It is part of your legacy. Never allow fear to prevent you from being your very best.

Living in New York City, one has ample opportunities to visibly recognize the haves and the haves not. Harlem was once known as the black cultural capital of the country. Theatres, churches, businesses and clubs stood in celebration of the Harlem Renaissance, which had occurred from 1917 to 1929.

In 2000, racial gentrification began to take place in historical Harlem. The white citizens of downtown quickly bought landmark brownstones, and businesses that were not owned by blacks. African - Americans had been the dominant citizens of the community for over ninety-years. Yet they owned less than 20% of the real estate in their community.

Harlemites had been renting their homes or business. They did not own them. Some of the black politicians had purchased property but had failed to alert their constituents about the need to own real estate in Harlem. Fast forward to 2008 - the majority of Harlem's real estate has been purchased by individuals with money and excellent credit. This does not include the black citizens who have resided for over nine decades.

Native Harlemites found themselves priced out of the market. They had simply been living day to day. They did not plan for their future in real estate. Understand, while you are snoozing others are planning. And their plans only involve how they are going to make money off of you-if you have any. Or how they are going to change the face of your community. Brownstones that sold for $300,000 in 1998 were now selling for 1.5 million in 2006. Abandoned buildings were quickly purchased by white developers and converted into condos and co-ops. The apartments were now priced at $650,000 for a two-bedroom apartment. Thus, pricing out the residents of Harlem.

Instead of being prepared for the changing of the guards, the citizens of Harlem demanded meetings to discuss what was happening. They failed to realize that the time for talking was over twenty years ago. And while they were waiting for an opportunity to voice their opinions, properties were being purchased throughout their community.

Earlier signs of gentrification came when communities that rarely saw a police presence began to notice a change. More and more police officers were walking the beat to ensure the safety of its citizens. Their presence had been missing before the changing of the guard was enacted in Harlem. Again, the residents insisted on meetings to discuss their dismay at the sudden appearance of police in their community. All to no avail. The fabric of Harlem had changed.
There are opportunities at every corner for an individual with a dream. You have to go for it and not be distracted by any obstacles in your path. You have to create a plan to get around all obstacles and work to achieve your goals.

The only thing you have to fear is fear itself. Move forward. Dare to dream. Do not worry about what others say. Determine your goals and do not stop until you reach them. Along the way assemble all tools necessary for the journey. Remember, it all begins with your education and your ability and pleasure of reading. The only obstacle in your path is you, and that should be easy to overcome. Additionally, Your mama should have told you that:

- Families have to establish traditions and cultural celebrations that connect to the work and achievements of our ancestors and family members.

- All families must read and study the lives of Frederick Douglass, Sojourner Truth, Harriet Tubman, Dr. W.E. B. Dubois, Madam C.J. Walker, Langston Hughes, Zora Neale Hurston, Marcus Garvey, Dr. Martin Luther King Jr., Malcolm X, Nelson Mandela, Dr. Ben Carson, and others. Their stories are those of success. They were rewarded after overcoming tremendous obstacles.
- Families must discover and discuss the contributions that were made by people of African-descent and celebrate the accomplishments daily.
- And, after we are finished researching and celebrating the 13 individuals above, we must seek out others like: Ossie Davis and Ruby Dee, Paul Robeson, Booker T. Washington, Hattie McDaniel, Bill "Bojangles" Robinson, Oprah Winfrey, Tyler Perry, Denzel Washington, Spike Lee, Wynton Marsalis, Cicely Tyson, Maya Angelou and others.

The award-winning documentary series *Eyes on the Prize*, and films *Malcolm X, Tuskegee Airmen, Rosewood, Glory, The Autobiography of Miss Jane Pittman, Amistad, Birth of a Nation (2016), Race,* and *Roots* should not be viewed only as vehicles for entertainment, but also as points of entry for family discussions and celebrations. Children should be guided to see themselves in the world and understand that their history is not only touched by slavery and racisms but by many other facets of accomplishments that are not as devastating. If parents do not work towards creating positive role models for their children-others will. And their motivation will be less about culture building, but rather as an impetus to pad their pockets while victimizing your child.

As we moved into 2023 and onwards it was determined that there was a need for a movement that addressed the onslaught of senseless deaths at the hands of police officers. The Black Lives Matter (BLM) movement became prolific and necessary. It has garnered support around the world. It was no longer acceptable to be fearful of the possible outcomes. Our had to be stifled and action was necessary to make an impact on the injustices that were inflicted upon African Americans.

Black Lives Matter

The Black Lives Matter movement has had a profound and far-reaching impact on society, igniting a global conversation about racial justice, police brutality, and systemic racism. Since its emergence in 2013, BLM has become a powerful force in the fight against racial inequality, advocating for the rights and dignity of Black individuals and communities.

One of the most significant contributions of the BLM movement has been its ability to raise awareness about the disproportionate violence and discrimination faced by Black people. Through protests, social media campaigns, and community organizing, BLM has drawn attention to the deep-rooted systemic issues that perpetuate racial injustice. The movement has compelled individuals, institutions, and governments to confront and address the pervasive racism that persists in various facets of society, including law enforcement, education, and healthcare.

BLM has also played a pivotal role in mobilizing people around the world. Its inclusive and intersectional approach has fostered solidarity among diverse communities, amplifying the voices of marginalized groups and highlighting the interconnectedness of various forms of oppression. The movement has provided a platform for individuals to share their stories, experiences, and demands for justice, challenging the status quo and demanding meaningful change.

Moreover, the impact of BLM extends beyond awareness and mobilization. The movement has catalyzed tangible policy reforms, such as the implementation of police accountability measures, the reevaluation of discriminatory practices, and the push for criminal justice reform. BLM's influence has permeated into cultural spaces as well, prompting discussions on representation, diversity, and inclusivity in media, arts, and entertainment.

The Black Lives Matter movement has sparked a seismic shift in public consciousness, shedding light on the persistent racial inequalities that continue to plague societies worldwide. By demanding justice, challenging systemic racism, and fostering dialogue and action, BLM has made an indelible impact on the fight for racial justice and equality. As the movement continues to evolve, its legacy serves as a reminder that the struggle for racial equality is an ongoing and collective responsibility that requires sustained effort and dedication from individuals and institutions alike.

The first step to solidifying freedom, justice, and equality begins with cultivating a healthy habit of reading. The next step requires placing educational attainment on its rightful pedestal from kindergarten to the completion of college. The third step is to nurture and support our families and communities. The final step requires the creation of a financial plan that eliminates support from governmental and social agencies and the development of generational wealth. The understanding and practice of these steps will initiate the overdue steps necessary for social justice. These factors will also serve to release the fear and begin you on the path to financial stability, good health, and generational wealth.

Summary
- This chapter delves into the history of fear within the African American community, stemming from a legacy of oppression, violence, and a fear of challenging the status quo.
- It discusses the fear that has been instilled through generations due to the assassination of leaders, lynching, and violence against African Americans.
- This fear has been perpetuated through history and has led to a reluctance to strive for excellence and success.
- The chapter highlights the importance of overcoming this fear and embracing a desire for success, education, and achievement.
- It emphasizes the need to recognize and reject the psychological fear that has been ingrained and to instead pursue greatness.

- The chapter discusses how history, including slavery and the civil rights movement, has shaped the African American psyche, and how this history can inform and inspire individuals to excel in spite of adversity.
- The chapter then profiles contemporary activists who have risen above fear to make significant impacts, including Amanda Gorman, Patrisse Cullors, Bryan Stevenson, Nipsey Hussle, and Stacey Abrams. Their stories serve as examples of individuals who have challenged the status quo, overcome fear, and made positive changes in their communities and society at large.
- Furthermore, the chapter emphasizes the importance of education, self-belief, and generational wealth-building as keys to overcoming fear and achieving success.
- It discusses the need for African Americans to create their own opportunities, rather than relying on external factors or government assistance.
- The chapter also highlights the Black Lives Matter movement and its role in addressing racial injustice and systemic racism, showing how collective action can lead to meaningful change.
- The chapter encourages readers to release fear, pursue education and success, and work towards building generational wealth, ultimately contributing to social justice and equality.
- It underscores the importance of breaking free from the psychological chains of fear and embracing a future of empowerment and achievement.

About the Author

Dr. Evelyn Collins stands as a distinguished and forward-thinking luminary in the realms of theater, African American History, and arts education, boasting an illustrious career that spans over three and a half decades. Throughout this journey, she has passionately committed herself to shaping and implementing innovative curricula, pioneering programs, and educational institutions with a resolute focus on the arts.

At the helm of the Onyx Production Company, Dr. Collins assumes the role of CEO, stewarding this professional organization in the creation of original works that beautifully reflect the rich tapestry of African American culture and experiences. Furthermore, Dr. Collins serves as the driving force behind the Harlem Ensemble Company, a non-profit theater collective renowned for its presentations of plays, musicals, and cinematic endeavors.

Dr. Collins' educational journey is a testament to her unwavering commitment to academic excellence. She has served as a principal, assistant principal, teacher, district administrator and adjunct instructor in New York City, Ann Arbor, Harlem and Mount Vernon.

Her educational credentials include a Doctorate in Education from Fordham University, specializing in Urban Education and School Leadership, a Master's degree in Directing for the Theatre from the University of Michigan, a Master of Science in Educational Leadership from the College of New Rochelle, and a Master of Fine Arts (candidate) in Theatre Management/Producing from Columbia University. She also holds a Bachelor of Arts degree in Theatre and Education from the University of Michigan, alongside a plethora of certifications in school leadership and administration.

Beyond her formidable academic and leadership roles, Dr. Collins shines as an accomplished author, captivating public speaker, and highly sought-after arts consultant. Notably, she has contributed a historical case study (dissertation –

Fordham University) on the Duke Ellington School of the Arts to the scholarly research. Her unwavering dedication to multicultural theater and her profound impact on the Harlem, Ann Arbor, and NYC communities have garnered her a multitude of awards and widespread recognition.

10 Things Your Mama Should Have Told You marks the beginning of a series of books created to support the edification and growth of all people.

www.ingramcontent.com/pod-product-compliance
Lightning Source LLC
Chambersburg PA
CBHW080454170426
43196CB00016B/2805